HOW TO LIVE & WORK IN AMERICA

In this Series

other titles in preparation

How To...

LIVE & WORK
IN AMERICA

Steve Mills

Northcote House

© *Copyright 1988 by Steve Mills*

First published in 1988 by Northcote House Publishers Ltd,
Harper & Row House, Estover Road, Plymouth PL6 7PZ, United
Kingdom.
Tel: Plymouth (0752) 705251. Telex: 45635. Fax: (0752) 777603.

British Library Cataloguing in Publication Data
Mills, Stephen
  How to live and work in America — (How to series).
  1. United States — Handbook, manuals, etc.
  I. Title
  917.3'04927   E158
  ISBN 0-7463-0330-0

Printed and bound in Great Britain

Contents

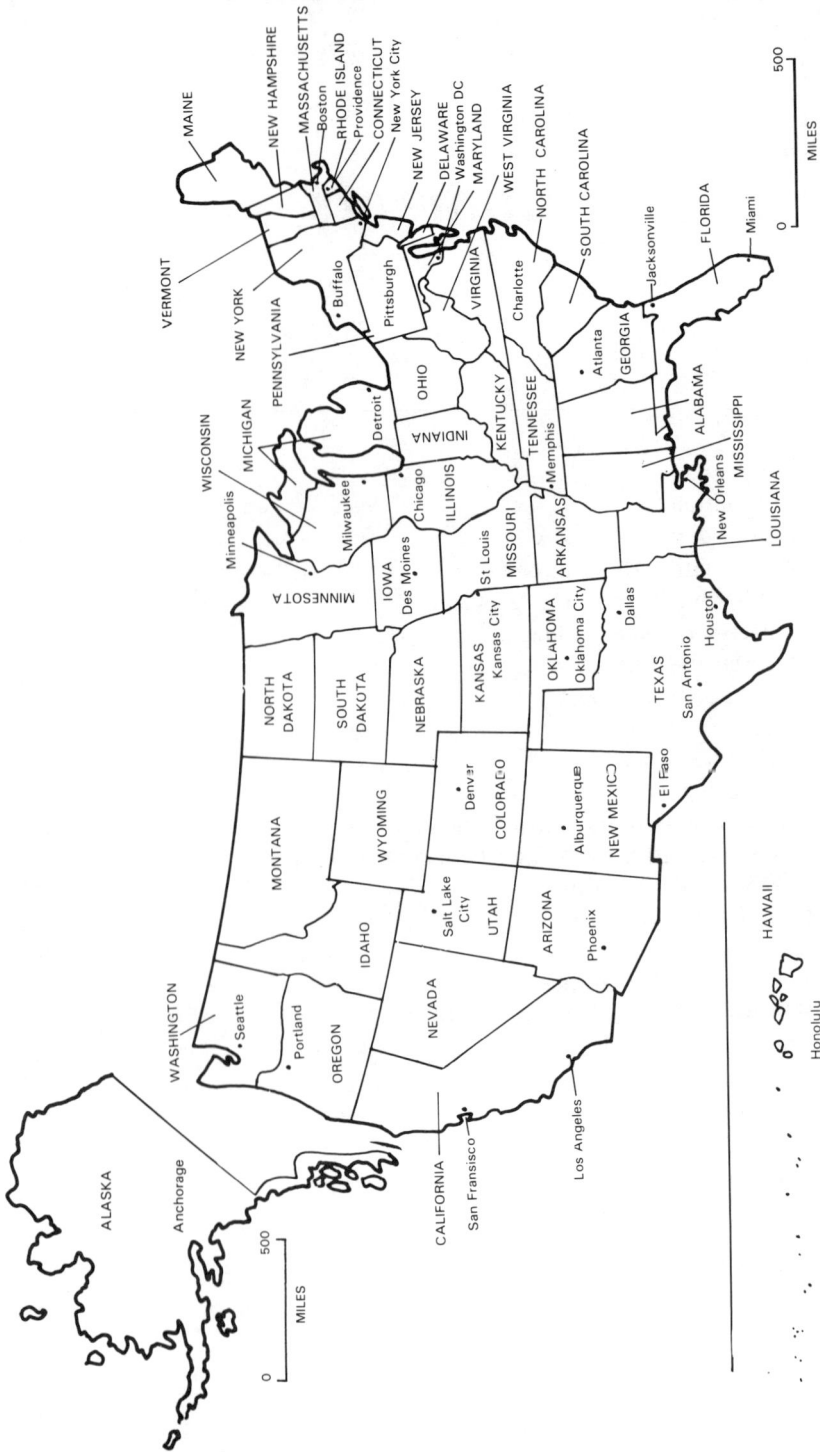

MAINE

NEW HAMPSHIRE
MASSACHUSETTS
Boston
RHODE ISLAND
Providence
CONNECTICUT
New York City
NEW JERSEY
DELAWARE
Washington DC
MARYLAND
WEST VIRGINIA
NORTH CAROLINA
SOUTH CAROLINA

VERMONT

NEW YORK

Buffalo

Pittsburgh

PENNSYLVANIA

VIRGINIA

Charlotte

Jacksonville

FLORIDA

Miami

MICHIGAN

WISCONSIN

Detroit

OHIO

INDIANA

KENTUCKY

TENNESSEE

Memphis

Atlanta

GEORGIA

ALABAMA

MISSISSIPPI

LOUISIANA

New Orleans

Minneapolis

Milwaukee

Chicago

ILLINOIS

MINNESOTA

IOWA

Des Moines

St Louis

MISSOURI

ARKANSAS

NORTH DAKOTA

SOUTH DAKOTA

NEBRASKA

KANSAS

Kansas City

OKLAHOMA

Oklahoma City

Dallas

TEXAS

San Antonio

Houston

MONTANA

WYOMING

Denver

COLORADO

Alburquerque

NEW MEXICO

El Paso

IDAHO

Salt Lake City

UTAH

ARIZONA

Phoenix

WASHINGTON

Seattle

Portland

OREGON

NEVADA

CALIFORNIA

San Franscisco

Los Angeles

HAWAII

Honolulu

ALASKA

Anchorage

500

MILES

0

500

MILES

0

Introduction

This is a book for anyone who has ever thought about spending some time in the United States. Millions of Europeans continue to go to the United States, whether for business or for pleasure, to visit or to stay, for anything from a long weekend to forever. Increasingly, though, the choice is not between a Concorde weekend break and emigration. Millions continue to visit the USA for a period longer than their annual holiday but without ever finally settling down there. This book is for anyone who has ever thought of living or working in the USA from a few weeks to many years. It is particularly geared at those who would like to experience the USA for more than just a few days holiday.

What follows results from living and working backwards and forwards across the Atlantic for the last 20 years, travelling from coast to coast by plane, by hitching, driving a van, by hired car, and even at times on foot. It's the result of visiting some 28 different States and living for five years in and around the Federal capital as much as of teaching American history, geography and urban studies to Britons and Americans at the University of Keele and the University of Maryland. It follows from entering the USA plane, by car, and even on foot, on three totally different kinds of visa, crossing sometimes alone, sometimes with family, on holiday and on business. It's a little bit of what has become American within me, even while I live and write in the UK.

I hope you will find the lessons of my own experience enable you, the reader, to enjoy your own visits to the USA with just a little more emphasis upon the fun and a little less on the hassle for having been that little more prepared than I ever was. Friends and colleagues have often said that I should pass on my experience: so here it is. With the incredible bits cut out so that you don't think this is another Tom Sharpe novel, here is a guide to living and working in the USA. May you enjoy your own experience as much as I've enjoyed mine.

SO WHAT DOES THIS BOOK DO?

It's a guide to the USA, providing hints and suggestions that may help you gain just that much more from your decision to visit or even to live USA. Many aspects of being in the USA come as a shock even for those who think they are well prepared. When I first arrived with a newly minted American Studies degree in my pocket I thought I'd arrived in the wrong country, so little did I recognise or understand in my first few weeks. So bad was the experience I could have cheerfully hijacked a plane out and away (in any direction!) if only I'd have known how. Nothing *bad* happened at all: no muggings, no illness, nothing specifically traumatic. But the *experience* overwhelmed me as I tried to cope with the reality of a new job, looking for somewhere to live, no car, no pay yet though my savings were fast ebbing away, and I'd arrived in one of the hottest and most humid Augusts for years. The only guides had been my textbooks and guidebooks for those visiting the sights. I didn't know that all the paper money was the same colour and size, that I'd have to pay a month's rent in advance plus a month's rent as deposit, that my pay wouldn't be paid directly into my account but that I'd have to do that myself every other Friday. Traffic on the right-hand side of the road was the least of my problems. That I'd expected!

HAVE A NICE DAY!

So this guide will start by asking you to consider what *you* expect from the USA, for what you want will be the most significant factor in how the USA measures up to your expectations. Anyone expecting a Big Mac in a vegetarian restaurant is going to get a nasty surprise! Be honest with yourself as to what you do want, and, just as importantly, what you don't want from a holiday, a family reunion, an American business market or a new start in life, and you'll be able to explore precisely what opportunities the USA does indeed hold for you.

Once you've decided you're off to the USA there's the whole question of the paperwork. The USA is not an easy country to deal with even once you've been let in. Many people expect US bureaucracy to be more efficient, or at least less convoluted than in Britain. They often find that the truth is far from pleasant. Whereas US visitors to Britain don't even need a visa, a UK visitor to the USA does, and so it goes on. And don't forget that everything governmental is duplicated: a State income tax may well be payable as well as the Federal one. Income tax liability is by self-assessment, but it's usually so complex, and the penalties threatened so dire, that most people pay a tax specialist to fill out the annual forms for them. Just thinking of your local tax inspector in Britain may bring a warm glow to your heart (but only while you're in the USA!).

But what opportunities exist? These are discussed in terms of the various groups − such as students, business people, entrepreneurs, professionals and artists. Read widely here, for though all face different problems all share similar problems as outsiders trying to get on the inside.

Throughout there is a wealth of information, outlining where best to go for further advice, with addresses and phone numbers for contacts both in Britain and in the USA. A careful use of the telephone can be a great time saver, especially in such a complex and potentially overwhelming matter as going to the USA.

CAVEAT

An economics lecturer once found himself required to teach a course he'd never taught before: the principles of free enterprise. Realising that principles need to be put into practice for their significance to be fully appreciated he called his new class together on the first day of term and offered them a bargain. He would, he said, sell them the grade of their choice. If they wanted an A grade that would cost $100, a B $75 and so on. Payment was to be in cash, and the offer would lapse at the end of the first meeting of the class. Thus, he announced, students would learn as never before the first basic principle of free enterprise: everything has its price (or, if you want something you've got to pay for it).

Some students duly paid up, and having already received their grades didn't see any reason to turn up at any more classes in that particular course. Come the end of the course those who had paid for their grades but who hadn't shown up subsequently found, to their horror, that they had failed the course. 'And that,' said the teacher, 'brings us to the second principle of free enterprise: "Let the buyer beware".'

All of which brings us to this: whilst every attempt has been made by the author to ensure that the information presented in this book is accurate at the time of going to press neither the author nor the publishers can accept any responsibility for any errors or omissions.

1
Considering the USA

WHY CONSIDER GOING TO THE USA?

The appeal of the United States is as varied as the country is vast. Millions have traditionally gone there to settle down. Nowadays more and more people visit the USA whether on holiday, to visit family or friends, on business or to study, as the 747s ply backwards and forwards across the Atlantic. For many people a particular visit has been greatly enhanced by combining a business trip with a holiday, a family reunion with travelling around, or using an initial holiday as the way to sample American life before making a commitment to stay longer. The country is so large and varied that a lifetime of visits would hardly exhaust its potentials; the USA is more a continent than the kind of country found in Europe.

The British have a long association with the United States. The eastern (Atlantic) coast States were once British colonies, though they broke away from the empire in the late eighteenth century. English is

---

American or English?
In Illinios the State language is deemed *American*, but more usually, as in California's 1986 language referendum, 'English' will do.

---

still the main language, long since adopted as America's own. The initial settlers of the north-eastern States were English Puritans (and the states they founded are still together called New England). English and Welsh Quakers founded Pennsylvania further down the coast. Inland the mountains were first settled by Ulster folk tired of defending Ireland for the Crown. In the south the English landowners and Scots soldiers, pioneers and convicts laid the foundation of a distinctively Anglo-Saxon, almost pro-British society, but one quite unlike that back in

Europe, for here a plantation economy was directly based upon the labour of African slaves.

The Founding Fathers of the American republic were essentially English gentlemen in rebellion, paradoxically, to protect their English rights against a despotic government far away in Britain. To the west their descendants carved out an empire dedicated to individual freedom, corporate growth and the Protestant work ethic, sweeping aside the native societies societies (and most other European settlers). When millions of Europeans then arrived at the end of the nineteenth century, not at first speaking English, a nation based firmly upon American experience was already in place, echoing only faintly its British origins. These immigrants created an urban and industrial society almost obliterating the rural British landscape and so recasting the language and the political system that the links with Britain became even more obscured. Even as immigrants learned in school that their new country spoke English and used the common law, their numbers and the needs of their new surroundings brought about a continual reworking of vocabulary and syntax, whilst their strident demands for action and protection recast both the legal and government systems. The British link became ever more submerged: the United States becomes ever more foreign.

The British and the Irish, alone amongst Europeans, are uniquely able to ignore the foreignness of America if they choose to do so. Though America remains a very distant foreign country whose ethnic variety is today more firmly rooted in Africa or eastern Europe than in Britain or Ireland, the shared language opens up the USA to English-speaking Europeans as for no others from the Old World. Add the considerable number of such people with friends already in America and the British and Irish can retain their links with the USA even while the USA at large looks elsewhere, particularly today across the Pacific.

Even as the USA nowadays looks far beyond Britain and Ireland the British and Irish look ever more avidly at the USA. Hollywood movies first brought the rich variety of US life across the Atlantic. Today

television continues that tradition. The very quantity of TV movies, documentaries and situation comedies brings both fantasy and daily life into everyone's homes. The USA is a country we visit passively every day, year in, year out. No wonder it often seems more familiar than even unvisited parts of our country, and beckons with the promise of exotic parts where the locals reassuringly speak English. The educated and skilled middle classes, already speaking English, can consider settling down in the USA, melting into the background as quickly or as slowly as they want, like East Germans in West Germany; no language barriers to put off all but the most stout-hearted as happens when the French and German middle classes look across the Atlantic. No wonder it is to the USA that so many British people turn for holidays, business, or to start a new life.

THERE'S SOMETHING FOR EVERYONE IN AMERICA

This may sound like little more than an ad man's copy, like a Texan boast, or just a piece of wishful thinking. The size, the physical contrast, the ethnic variety, the particular rural-urban mix, the wealth and poverty and 400 years of European history (resting upon thousands of years of earlier people's!) means that whatever your interest, from landscape painting to railway trains, from ornithology to folk music, there is indeed something for everyone. And millions of British people have families over there, sisters and aunts who went over as GI brides in the 1940s, or brain drain scientists from the days of the space race.

It's amazing how many people have never visited their families in the USA but have always thought they'd like to, always able to find a 'reason' for not going.

HAVE YOU EVER THOUGHT...?

- **I haven't the time**
  Well, save up your annual leave. Most of us now get two weeks, and three can usually be arranged if planned far enough ahead.

- **I couldn't afford the money**
  It's not all the QE2, caviare and dressing for dinner now. Wide-bodied jets fly across in eight hours for only a couple of hundred pounds if you can book a month or so in advance.

- **They've never asked me over**
  They probably did years ago, or thought they did. Why not ask if they'd like to come visit you? That would get the ball rolling!

- **I don't like all that violence you see on TV**
  Though Washington DC is more violent than Belfast most visitors never see anything more violent than a repeat episode of *Blott on the Landscape* on American TV. If you are sensible and are staying with family or friends, visiting the USA is less dangerous than staying at home. And US sports crowds are very well behaved!

- **I couldn't stand all the junk food**
  Fast food isn't the only food the US is famous for. Every kind under the sun is available (even fish and chips, from equipment made in Britain!). This is hardly surprising given all the different people (from Albanians to Vietnamese) who have settled there over the years.

- **I wouldn't like the heat**
  The US has taken central heating in winter and air conditioning in summer to its heart. You need only be hot (or cold) if you want to be.

- **I hate motorway travel**
  Well fly, or take the train (yes, long distance trains still connect the main cities with some degree of civilisation). Also, believe it or not, driving an air-conditioned mid-size hired car can be almost relaxing at a continuous 55 mph over the gently graded freeways of the south and west, with a comfortable motel at the day's end (including a swim in the pool followed by a steak supper and a film on the TV movie channel in your room).

NO RELATIVES IN THE USA?

- **Well find some!**
  Didn't a cousin go over, marry and stay? Now's the chance to visit that aunt you've not seen since Christmas 1973 to ask her about her daughter in Seattle. Doesn't someone have a US penfriend from days in the Scouts?

- **Old school friends?**
  Ring around and find who's gone abroad. An old school friend now in Alberta would give you somewhere to aim for as you drive westwards from Chicago. A trip just across the border would be quite interesting, and a worthwhile detour *en route* for Seattle!

- **Ask around...**
  for people at school, college, work or sports club who have been to the USA. They may have US friends who keep open house to visiting stamp collectors, squash players, local historians, bird

watchers and so on. How would you respond if an American couple who shared your passion for bees or real ale wrote saying they were passing through your area on their next holiday? Wouldn't you get the spare room ready and take the risk of inviting in strangers on the basis of a mutual friend and a shared hobby?

- **Ask at your school, college, rotary meeting...**
  about people who have gone on sponsored visits, scholarships and exchanges. Track them down and ask them how they arranged to go over, what it cost, who they stayed with. They'll probably be only too pleased to share their experiences with you.

Most of us can get to visit the USA one way or another if we are employed (or students with job prospects). It may take a year or so of overtime saving up the money or a couple of long vacations pulling pints in a holiday resort, and if you want to give up smoking or drinking a trip to the USA would be a worthwhile target to save for, and something to get you through the cravings. Some people have even taken to entering competitions as a hobby, and once into the swing of things, they start to recognise what's required of entries and tie-breaking slogans, winning prizes that can include holiday trips abroad. It's a long shot, but some-one's going to win that trip by Concorde for two to Disneyland. It could just be you!

LISTING YOUR INTERESTS IN THE USA

Make your own list, for example:

- touring the sights
- going on a resort-based family holiday
- visiting friends or relatives
- going on a speciality trip (battlefields, bird watching, old cars)
- making a business trip
- having a look around prior to emigrating

All are excellent reasons for going to the USA. But if you can make it clear in your own mind why you are interested in the USA then it'll be easier to answer the essential question:

What do I/we want from our trip to the USA?

You may well be able to combine several concerns

- visiting family then touring
- family holiday after a business visit
- family resort plus personal speciality
- touring between business visits

•

Beware!

Mixing your trips together could ruin the whole thing:

- What would happen if the children got sick while you are all hurrying to the next business appointment?
- Will the children be able to enjoy anything on a rapid, long distance chase between business appointments?
- What will you do if friends not seen for years now chain-smoke, wife shop, play bridge all the time, are workaholics or can't stand children?

However, some considerations can work out just fine:

- if you are geared up to tour you can make your excuses and leave any disastrous reunion;
- if militant chain-smoking friends have now mellowed with children and exercise you can always stay a night longer than planned, or even visit again on your way back to the airport.

WHAT KIND OF VISIT DO YOU WANT?

For some people holidays are action-packed, for others relaxed and gentle. Where you go depends upon how you feel about holidays:

	like	*so-so*	*don't like*
Big cities like New York			
Resorts such as Disneyworld			
Famous sights or battlefields			
Spectacular landscapes			
Lakes and forests			

Using a different coloured pen, go over an make the choices again, this time thinking how your children might respond. Then ask your children to fill in *their* choices: did you get their choices right? Did they like the choices you'd already made for them?

Would you gain relaxation from visiting the following?

	yes	don't know	no
Manhattan's shops			
Niagara Falls			
Washington's museums			
Virginia's battlefields			
Casinos of Las Vegas			
Disneyworld			

If you've built up a column of no answers, then for a relaxing holiday you may need to go elsewhere, or perhaps concentrate upon some US version of what you've done successfully before:

- If you like walking in the Lake District...
  try walking in the Rocky Mountain National Park.
- If you like the Costa del Sol...
  try the Florida coast around Miami.
- If you like Blackpool and Alton Towers...
  try Disneyworld.
- If you like the British Museum...
  try Washington DC's Smithsonian Institute.
- If you like the Normandy battlefields...
  try the Civil War battlefields.

To know what kind of visit you want you must sort out your priorities in your own mind. Remember, people who like the Lake District often like Blackpool too. But such a person might find one day at a resort quite enough, a week in the hills not enough. If you want mountains, with a day off in a resort then don't go to Florida, for unlike Britain the drive from resort to mountains isn't an hour up the motorway, but two whole days! If you make a mistake in the USA you may well be stuck with it, though no more perhaps than if you'd flown off to the Mediterranean.

FUTHER THOUGHTS ON STAYING WITH FRIENDS OR RELATIVES

It's worth thinking how well you relax with friends and relatives *back home* before you visit overseas.

- Do you dread visiting your wife/husband's school friends?
- Do you now find your old college friends boring?
- Do you leave Aunty Flo's as soon as possible?
- Do you leave your in-laws' vowing never to return?

If family visits are fraught with suppressed anger at home perhaps you ought to reconsider such an option overseas!

Also consider

- **How well** do you know your old friends and relatives?
- Have your **holiday demands** changed since you all last met?
- What **options** do you have if their welcome sours?
- Can you afford to **risk** your family holiday or business trip?

A leisurely week on a canal boat on North Staffordshire's Cauldon Canal with a couple of days at the Alton Towers leisure park plus canalside real ale and cream teas would be a more relaxing way to spend your hard-earned holiday if family and one-time friends simply get you het up rather than help you relax

But you can always keep your options open. If there's any doubt about staying with family or friends in the USA make them just one part of a tour around. Knowing that you'll be off and away in a couple of days can help you relax and may make all the difference between a successful and a disastrous trip.

FAMILY REUNIONS

Family reunions can be short or long. A short stay with friends or relatives in Britain can turn out to be little short of a disaster. Imagine how awful it would be to leave Britain to spend the rest of your days with your family already long settled in the USA only to find out after a few weeks that you can't stand each other. If you intend to live with, or even nearby, younger family it's essential that:

- it's been thought through carefully by *all* concerned;
- you've visited and seen what accommodation is available;
- everyone knows what the financial implications will be (will grand-parents' pensions from Britain be sufficient to keep them, or will a family subsidy be necessary?);
- you must have talked over and experienced each other's lifestyles in case the clash is too loud;

- each side should know and understand their responsibilities (from paying rent to baby-sitting).

Initially the most crucial thing is for the Europeans to visit and stay with the Americans. And stay beyond the holiday couple of weeks. Anyone can put up with almost anyone for a few weeks. But how about after three months? What is it like in the middle of a midwestern winter? — a Florida summer? Parents do go overseas to be with their grown-up children, and it can be the start of a very successful new life. But it can also be a recipe for disaster. But then staying at home never seeing children and grandchildren isn't always much fun either.

A word of warning
A family holiday in, say, Florida can be quite expensive, even though you may get value for money and a holiday to remember. But if you dwell too much on how much it's costing you may be driven to cram in too many people and places to get your money's worth.

- Just think of a generation of US visitors that have done precisely that ('If it's Tuesday it must be Belgium').
- Trying to see everything, even in one State, will mean an awful lot of time will be spent on the motorway (whether on the bus or in a hired car). Would you advise Americans to see as much of Britain as possible by way of keeping to the M4, M5, M6, M74, A1(M) and M1 circuit? And yet Britain is smaller than most US States!
- If you visit a Florida relative it doesn't mean you will be able to drive to visit others in New Orleans, Chicago and New York City, even though on a map that looks like a reasonable drive around. Would you spend a continental holiday driving from home to Moscow and back again by way of Athens? If this visit to the USA is indeed the trip of a lifetime and you really must see everyone then consider flying instead. **Multiple destination tickets** can be arranged before leaving home, often in conjunction with your transatlantic carrier, at very advantageous rates. If you must drive either take as long as possible so that you can leave the motorways, visiting as you go along, or better still, plan to come back again to visit the rest of the family.

2
Alternative Destinations

If you want to experience life in another part of the English-speaking world, the United States is not the only country you might like to consider, whether for a visit or to live. English is spoken in many countries, each of which offers both families and individuals a wide range of alternatives, from a place to relax to a fresh start in a new home.

Just considering alternatives to the USA may help sort out precisely what you're looking for in going abroad. You may end up knowing that the USA *is* for you after all!

CANADA

Larger than the USA, but with only about half Britain's population, Canada is a bilingual country where English *and* French are equal in the eyes of the law. The British-settled Maritime provinces on the Atlantic coast are today far from economically buoyant, relying upon federal aid, tourism and fishing. The dynamic areas of English-speaking Canada are now further inland, from Toronto on the Great Lakes westwards to Vancouver on the Pacific coast, especially the rich farm lands and oil of the prairies around Calgary. French-speaking Canada, once restricted mainly to the farmland along the St Lawrence River, is now both urban and industrial, based upon Montreal and its massive iron ore fields and electrical generating stations to the north.

After a prolonged visit to the USA English-speaking Canada may appear very British, though if arriving directly from Europe it'll likely appear very American with its sprawling cities, freeways, high summer humidity and deep winter chills. Increasingly cosmopolitan Canada retains for many visitors and residents alike the benefits of the old world in the new. Does it really have all the benefits of the USA but with few of the problems?

Getting there
- Similar air packages exist as for the USA
- The British Visitor's Passport is valid (though *not* for cross border trips to the USA)
- No visas are required for tourists up to 90 days
- For long stays first contact the Canadian authorities *before* leaving home.

Staying there
- As the recession tightened in the late 1970s immigration restriction became more stringent. Permission to live in Canada, 'landed immigrant status', became available only to certain people with specific skills needed but not locally available. *This principle is rigorously applied.*

- Temporary work for foreign visitors is generally *not* allowed. Male students are, however, permitted to apply for a permit to work on tobacco farms in southern Ontario (contact **British Universities North America Club**, 58/60 Berners Street, London W1, for details. Early application is essential). Casual jobs for cash are likely to be in fruit-picking in the Okanagan Valley of British Columbia, or in the bars of the Rocky Mountain resorts.

- Immigration and visa enquiries should be made initially at the **High Commission,** 38 Grosvenor Street, London W1 ((01) 409 2071).

Considering Canada?

	yes	no
I don't mind no sub-tropical or desert areas		
Speaking in French would be fun		
I quite like the British heritage		
I like cities that aren't dangerous		
I'd enjoy harsh winters 'with all mod cons'		

If you've answered *yes* to three or more then further consideration of Canada seems a good idea. But you could be based in Canada and drive to sub-tropical or desert areas. You could ignore, by where you are, either the French or the British heritage, or even both! You could also enjoy Canada-like conditions (social, economic and climatic!) across large parts of the USA, for instance in the harsh but anticipated winters of Minnesota.

Reconsidering the USA

- Don't think the USA is all New York City, Miami and Los Angeles. Small town America has been making a comeback these last few years, with some very high growth rates. It isn't all *Hill Street Blues* and *Miami Vice.*
- If you settle in the USA Canada is there as a great place to visit.
- The US economy is generally more vibrant, and for the real go-getter the USA remains the place to be in certain fields such as the movies or rock music.

Perhaps the phrase should be 'There's something for everybody in North America'?

But perhaps you would like to consider ever further afield before making your choice of destination? Let's consider first the other old Dominions.

AUSTRALIA

Another federal, mainly English-speaking country-cum-continent where every state is a very large Texas-like slice. Most people live around the coast, especially in the south-east within the Brisbane-Sydney-Adelaide arc. Tourism from Europe (and North America) is being actively encouraged to supplement the dwindling family reunion trade.

The people are more cosmopolitan than you might expect (especially Yugoslavs and Italians in the big cities). Many see this as part of an Americanisation of Australia. The outback remains virtually uninhabited, as per *Crocodile Dundee,* a vast continent much like the deserts of Utah, Arizona and New Mexico. Distances are immense, so plan accordingly.

Getting there

Visitors have to travel halfway around the globe to get there, so round the world trips are a distinct possibility, and if coordinated with family

Beware: if your US stopover is in Los Angeles don't expect relatives from Miami, Florida, or even Seattle, Washington to come to visit you. Would you go to greet a visiting American relative on their arrival in Rome, never mind Istanbul?

and friends *en route,* say in Canada or the USA, the stopovers can be put to good use. But you must ensure that stopovers are where you'd want them to be, with enough time before flying on.

Moving there
The days of the £10 passage are long gone. Immigrants must fill specific jobs or meet other strict criteria. Many Australian firms, though, still actively recruit in Britain, and the various state governments still retain their individual offices in London to complement the Australian High Commission.

- The **High Commission** is in Australia House, The Strand, London WC2. For immigration forms call (01) 836 7123. For temporary entry or visitors visas call (01) 836 7161.

- Australian universities recruit through **The Association of Commonwealth Universities,** 36 Gordon Square, London WC1 ((01) 387 8572).

NEW ZEALAND

New Zealand was once deemed more British than Britain, though now more cosmopolitan, more aware of its Maori heritage, and increasingly aware that Britain has long since turned away to NATO and the EEC for defence and trade. Nevertheless many British families still settle here, and visits are increasingly feasible, especially for those with time to stay down under, such as pensioners visiting grown-up children.

The scenery is spectacular. The South Island Alps have glaciers that emerge through towering peaks into sub-tropical forest. The North Island is more tropical, less mountainous, and more Maori. Miles of beaches and coves await the visitor. The contrast with Australia's dry desert interior is stark.

Getting there
As for Australia, round the world tickets can mean visits down under can be by way of family and friends in North America for very little extra, given adequate planning schedules.

Moving there
Emigration from Britain these days is usually in response to specific job recruitment. New Zealand firms, corporations and universities still advertise in the British popular and specialist press.

- The **High Commission** is at New Zealand House, Haymarket, London SW1 ((01) 930 8422).

SOUTH AFRICA

South Africa was once a major British destination. The Mediterranean climate, a high standard of living, and the scenic beauty still attract many visitors and immigrants from Britain. Those wishing to settle are especially sought after, if only to counter-balance those South Africans who are leaving this troubled land.

Most people here are denied the vote. Stringent anti-terrorist laws override any veneer of democratic safeguards generally enjoyed in western Europe, North America, Australia and New Zealand. All male residents including recent arrivals are liable to be called up into the Defence Force, and may well see action in occupied Namibia or in the townships such as Soweto. Those able to emigrate will do so without most of their assets which must be left behind.

But the beaches along the Indian Ocean are magnificent. National Parks are world famous. The food and wine are good. Servants are cheap. And state censorship means that almost no word of the civil war reaches the ears of white residents via television, radio or the press.

- Further details from **RSA Embassy,** South Africa House, Trafalgar Square, London Wc2 (immigration: ((01) 839 2211).

Since the 1950s the UK has turned away from its former Commonwealth partners towards the rest of Europe. If you wish to take advantage of this changing situation consider working on the continent.

THE EEC

In theory the free movement of goods, services and people within the countries of the community should encourage nationals of any one community country to consider working rather than just holiday-making in any of the others. Language and red tape, however, mean otherwise. Professional qualifications are rarely interchangeable, and language requirements keep out all but the bilingual.

The community offices in Strasbourg, Luxembourg and Brussels are required, however, to hire from all community countries, but many posts are by secondment from member government, or require translation skills in at least two community languages other than one's own. Word has it that the skill to have these days is to be able to translate Danish into Greek.

The International Baccalaureate is an attempt to provide a common matriculation qualification for bilingual, often diplomats' children, but as yet it has little popular currency. Middlesex Polytechnic runs a four-year sandwich BA (Honours) in European Business Administration in conjunction with French, German and Spanish degree-giving institutions, an internationally recognised qualification backed by appropriate business and language skills.

- Contact: **Middlesex Polytechnic (Admissions)**, 114 Chase Side, London N14 5PN. ((01) 886 6599 − 24 hours for general information);
- Or: **Middlesex Business School,** The Burroughs, London NW4 4BT. ((01) 202 6545 for more specific enquiries).

OTHER OVERSEAS OPPORTUNITIES

The EEC and the old dominions are not the only possible alternatives to living and working in the United States.

- At your next job interview ask what opportunities exist for overseas work. At least it'll give you something to say when the interviewer asks 'Any questions?'

- **Teaching English as a Foreign Language (TEFL)**
  If you wish to live abroad, from Brazil to Japan, this might be a worthwhile investment of time and money. These courses are *not* grant aided. If you already have a teaching certificate and a degree in English this added qualification could be profitable. The quality newspapers, such as the *Guardian's* Tuesday education section, have adverts for colleges offering TEFL (postgraduate) courses. Many of the good colleges attempt placements for their successful students. For those with a degree or teaching qualification plus a recognised TEFL qualification *plus* at least one year's TEFL experience details of overseas posts can be obtained from **Overseas Educational Appointments Department,** The British Council, 65 Davies Street, London W1Y 2AA.

- **Voluntary Service Overseas (VSO)**
  The old image of spending a year in voluntary service overseas before going on to college is still around, but for the most part VSO prefers graduates with practical skills like home economics, animal husbandry or intermediate technology. And it is not restricted to the 18 to 22 group with a year to kill. In fact contracts can be for several years so that worthwhile projects can be undertaken. Contact: **VSO** at 9 Belgrave Square, London SW1 ((01) 235 5191).

- **Charities**
  Organisations like Oxfam send people overseas, though these are likely to be people who have worked their way up through the system (from initially helping in a shop up to the Oxford HQ), or who are sent to target projects with highly developed, often managerial, skills. People with degrees in Development Studies might just possibly have an edge over other people in getting into the aid business.

3
What's It Like in the USA?

Americans know an awful lot about Britain and Ireland. They see the royal weddings on breakfast television and the latest bombed RUC police station on the nightly news. Avidly they watch the Dickensian horrors of *Nicholas Nickleby,* delight in the decadent affluence of *Brideshead Revisited* or thrill to the period pieces of Agatha Christie's rural detective mysteries. The Sherlock Holmes stories forewarn a further generation about London fog while *Blott on the Landscape* confirms stereotypes of a perverted, class-conscious old world. It's hardly surprising the real thing often comes as a great surprise to American visitors.

European misconceptions about the USA may be just as misleading, for our images come from a steady diet of musicals and horror films, cop adventure shows and such modern swashbuckling yarns as the *A-Team* and *Starsky and Hutch.* Unfortunately these media images repel as many people as they attract. Endless violence, materialism, urban sprawl and drugs seem to cloud many people's views, as do equally misleading images of easy wealth, limitless opportunity, and beautiful weather.

Stereotypes

• All US television is endless soap operas, commercials and cop shows.	But	• Many stations are free of commercials within specific programmes – especially cable channels and publicly financed stations.
• America is just too violent to visit let alone live in.	But	• Sport is family entertainment with spectator violence almost unheard of.
• The New York City subway system is dangerous and very difficult for visitors to understand.	But	• The Washington DC metro system is one of the world's safest and cleanest, and it's easy to use.

- Everything is so much   But • Petrol is 90p a gallon.
  more expensive in the
  USA. Everyone knows
  that!

Of course each stereotype can be substantiated. Commercial television
can seem impossibly overloaded with adverts, the USA is considerably
more violent than Britain or Northern Ireland, and though cheap the
New York City subway is indeed chaotic, under-capitalised and the
scene of much violence. But if you are prepared to look more widely the
stereotypes can be put into some kind of perspective. After all the USA
is almost a continent, with some 240,000,000 people of every kind.
Knowing a little about where to go and what to avoid, what to buy and
what not to, can make all the difference.

For most would-be visitors the outstanding feature will probably be
the USA's great variety of people and places, plus the incredible extremes of wealth.

THE USA: PEOPLE AND PLACES

The USA is about half of North America, one of the world's major
continents, over 9 million square kilometres (some $3\frac{1}{2}$ million square
miles). Today the USA stretches beyond the mainland 48 states to the
Arctic wastes of northern Alaska and the tropical forests of Hawaii.
There is also one Federal district (Washington DC), plus the Caribbean
Commonwealth of Puerto Rico and assorted island colonies. Being
mostly temperate with but little of the polar or equatorial extremes
found in other countries such as Canada or the USSR on the one hand
or Brazil or Zaire on the other, the USA is one of the most fertile slices
of any continent anywhere.

During the nineteenth century the newly independent USA spread
westwards from its original colonial toe-hold along the Atlantic coast,
over the mountains and rivers of the continental interior to the Pacific.
This produces an essential feature of American geography: the
mountains, rivers, weather systems and even migrating birds tend to
move north and south, but the USA spreads against and across the
grain. The attempt to forge a great north-south trading system to exploit
the lay of the land and the southward movement of the main river
system failed when the Mississippi River lost out to the growing east-
west railway networks last century. Nevertheless, the overall physical
structure of the USA remains north-south.

To the east are the Appalachian Mountains, long worn down to mere
stumps, though high enough (Mt Mitchell is over 2,000 m high!), wide
enough and forested enough to thwart generations of settlers until new
travel technologies opened up such gaps as existed. The Mississippi

interior was opened up originally by military adventurers, explorers, and finally traders. Settlers soon carved up the grasslands into some of the most fertile farms ever created. Miners carried the sweep into the Rockies of the Far West. Not one range, but a whole series of mountains and basins, these western ranges contain both the highest point in the country, outside Alaska, Mt Whitney (4,418 m) and the lowest, Death Valley (−86 m).

The vast interior desert between the Rocky Mountain front ranges in Colorado and the Sierra Nevada mountains of California is so isolated that it was here the Mormons were finally able to establish their new Promised Land last century. So out of this world is the landscape that in these barren wastes NASA's moonbuggy practice took place in the 1960s.

> When the NASA moonbuggy training was underway a passing Navajo Indian shepherd asked what they were doing. When he heard that they were bound for the moon he asked to record a message for any Navajo already on the moon. His recorded message for the lunar Navajo was finally translated. It simply said: 'Sign nothing'.

To the south the States of the Gulf of Mexico are vast areas of fertile farmlands, once covered with forests in the east, grasslands to the west. Hot and humid for much of the year, snow and ice are a rare surprise. Once inhabited by settled, farming native Indian peoples these areas were cleared in the 1830s for European settlement. African slaves were brought in to work the expanding cotton plantations. The Indians were driven into the barren areas across the border, later to become reservations under US control. Only in the western deserts could the native peoples survive on their traditional lands, as near the Grand Canyon, though hedged around by the US authorities.

As the USA expanded westwards to the Pacific the country changed economically and socially. From a once rural society of farms and small towns emerged an industrial giant of huge cities. Factories that both provided the rails and barbed wire for the western farmlands and required the increasing bounty of foodstuffs and raw materials needed more labour than the USA could provide. People poured in from all over Europe. Where once they had originally come mainly from Britain and similar northern European societies they now also flooded in first from Ireland, then from Italy, Poland and Russia, Jews and gentiles alike.

The USA today is only superficially a child of the British Isles. Rather, today's American people come from mainly continental stock, the torrent of urban and entrepreneurial peoples that flooded in before the First World War. Trade and manufacturing of an unprecedented scale developed, linking the products of the US interior with the wider world. Mostly east and southern European, these immigrants took up American English only in so far as it gave them access to political and economic power, plus social clout. They preserved the skin of America, but totally changed its core, not so much becoming Americans as changing the definition of what it was to be American.

The 1860s Civil War population of 40 million rose to over 100 million by the First World War. By then it was too late for the older America to turn back the tide. The immigrants, and particularly their children, had created a society so buoyant, so materially prosperous that they could now simply ignore much of this older, rural America of the Midwest High Plains and the Bible Belt. The brash society of the cities had little time for and even less contact with the increasingly resentful survivors of the countryside. Sometimes the White Anglo-Saxon Protestant (WASP) countryside would fight back, such as in pushing through the outlawing of alcohol (prohibition) and voting to end further mass immigration. But with an ever larger proportion of consumers and voters living and working in the cities such measures were far too late. The cities were liberal, pluralist, atomistic, and comparatively secular. The countryside remained WASP, small town, devout and outraged.

THE WEATHER

Where you decide to stay or to live may well depend purely upon what holiday packages or jobs are available. But the USA is so vast it helps to know what you may be letting yourself in for. The weather in the USA is not something that dominates conversation, as in Britain, but the extremes are such that the weather cannot be ignored completely except by the foolhardy.

The USA is continental in scale. The climate is as varied as you would find across all of Europe, from the Arctic north to the desert south. Much of western Europe is surrounded by water, whether the Atlantic or its North Sea, Baltic or Mediterranean offshoots. Though the USA is surrounded by the Atlantic, the Gulf of Mexico, the Pacific and the Great Lakes, vast areas are far from any influences from the oceans. The result is great extremes, not just in the interior but even along many coastal regions which are themselves influenced as much by the land mass behind them as by the waters offshore. It can easily be 43°C (100°F) or −40°C (− 40°F too!).

Summers are generally hot, and may be very humid as warm wet air moves northwards from the Caribbean. Winters can be as harsh as any in the inhabited world. In between these extreme seasons hurricanes or tornadoes inflict many areas where great air masses collide. Only in Maine, the Pacific northwest and perhaps Wisconsin can anything approaching a northern European summer be experienced.

The Pacific northwest alone will seem familiar to a visiting Brit in winter. The recurrent deep snows of New York City would be more familiar to a resident of Moscow than Lisbon or Rome. Los Angeles has a generally Mediterranean climate, Denver the climate of the Russian steppes, New Orleans and Washington DC a humid subtropical climate similar to that of Hong Kong (though fortunately without quite so much rain). Yuma in southwest Arizona has less rain than Alice Springs in Australia's central desert, and Miami has a tropical climate similar to that of Kisangani on the Congo River. Alaska is much like Scandinavia in both climate and topography.

Midwest warning
In **summer** the weather of the Midwest can be quite confusing. This vast expanse from the Rockies to the Great Lakes can be dull, grey and overcast, but usually it will also be very hot and humid, though the windy city Chicago can manage at times to be as cold and uninviting as any British seaside resort in a poor summer. In **winter,** however, the Arctic air sweeping down from Canada can make the Midwest treacherous, with chill factors (temperatures plus the wind-induced extra chilling effect) being well below zero. A blue sky in winter means heat loss, and so sunburn *and* hypothermia are both possible without care. Minus 40°C is not uncommon on the Prairies where six months earlier it could have been plus 40°C. Those not adequately prepared for these extremes will, and do, perish. Appropriate hats are worn in all seasons.

Winters are generally colder and longer than in Britain, with the possible exception of those areas around the Gulf of Mexico, around the southern Appalachians and along the Pacific coast. Be prepared for more snow, more ice, and more chilling winds than in island Britain. The bad winter Britain gets once every 20 years is fairly standard over much of the USA every year, even those areas of the interior so hot in summer. If you are used to crossing the Scottish Highlands on the A9 in

Seeing a sprinkling of snow this intrepid writer left home an hour earlier than usual to walk to his new job which started at 8 am, only to find the university closed: a 'snow alert' had been called. Always listen to the radio or watch breakfast TV for such announcements.

winter you will be quite at home in an American winter, drifts and all. But in the USA heating in homes and buildings, public and private, tends to be appropriate for the seasons, if not excessive. Be prepared to strip off into summer things if spending long in such places. Wear padded clothing if possible out of doors, even if you feel stupid looking like an explorer. Hats, gloves and boots are essential for survival, as is the ability to recognise when things are too bad to travel.

Summers are generally hotter, which is okay in the dry and often high southwest, but can be very sticky elsewhere. Air conditioning in a car is not really a luxury if it means that you arrive able to work, or if it means families can survive long journeys. Sceptical hard types will say: 'Just open the window!' Fine, but don't expect to be able to breathe what comes in. And try being a backseat passenger rather than an upfront driver for a while – you will soon get air conditioning.

The only snag is that much air conditioning can be fierce. Take a pullover or sweatshirt with you to work, to the movies, even to the supermarket or art gallery. For an interesting summer experience watch a summer movies (such as *Jaws*) in the chilly air conditioning of a movie theatre. To get the full effect stay dressed for the 35°C weather outside.

When first arriving in a hot and humid summer the temptation is to spend as much time as possible wherever air conditioning can be found, loitering over the shopping, developing a passion for great works of art or the movies. Assuming this doesn't give you a summer cold this 'cure' can make the problem worse if it means failing to come to terms in some way or another with the problem. A change in behaviour may well be called for, if only keeping out of the sun, walking in the shadow of high buildings, and taking plenty of liquids. Of course if children start to pass out waiting in the lines at Disneyworld, which happens, then you need to get them into the nearest air conditioned room. But wearing a hat, not sitting out in the sun, and lots of drinks may be necessary drills for all the family.

Air conditioning, however, has meant that lots of people from the North have been able to face moving to the sunbelt in search of work and retirement. The telephone system has helped integrate the South into the nation at large. People and businesses can now keep in touch wherever they are.

WHERE TO STAY

The range is enormous, from the cheap flea-pit to the luxury resort. Hotels are more expensive than motels, which tend to be more uniform in facilities and price.

Motels
Motels have two double beds, toilet and shower, plus a television as standard, often with cable TV, and a pool (although you must check there is a pool especially at the bottom end of the market). In summer 1987 prices started at about £35 ($60) per night, but prices are per room not per person, so for families or groups of friends this is good value. The Trust House Forte motel chain in the UK is the nearest in price and facilities to the US norm. Breakfast is not included, though ice may be (or available for a nominal 25c). Chains exist for a variety of price levels. **Best Western** and the **Holiday Inn** are more plush, and more pricey than **Motel 6** or **Econolodge. Howard Johnston's** have built-in coffee shops. Most motels don't have food service, but fast food outlets and family restaurants are usually next door, often with a discount arrangement if you show your key when paying the bill.

B & B
Bed and breakfast establishments do exist, but are usually accessible only through published lists, and are generally quite expensive if not Yuppie ('Sloane'). Over the border Canadian b & b's are more common, and put out 'Tourist Accommodation' signs to attract the casual visitor, especially in resorts such as Niagara Falls.

Good news

The mid 1980s saw a massive amount of motel construction, leading to a series of price wars. This means that in towns with an overabundance of motel construction chains may reduce their prices below that charged elsewhere. Check their prices on the huge bill boards visible from the main roads, phone, or just drop in and ask.

Also, much of this new construction has been to catch trade passing along the new roads, freeways and bypasses. The older motels on the older, now bypassed, roads are often far cheaper and may well have bargains, like special mid-week prices. These can be considerable saving (if you can avoid thinking of *Psycho*).

Self-catering
Self-catering apartments are common in the USA. These have all the mod-cons that you would expect in any motel (double beds, shower,

TV, phone, etc) plus as standard a fully fitted kitchen with dishwasher. It's unlikely that any other services would be available, like room service, but a coffee shop may well be part of the complex, or merely next door or across the street. Expect to pay at least £55 ($90) per night for a one-bedroom apartment, £100 ($160) per night for a two-bedroom suite sleeping 4 people. It is usually of course cheaper to stay in a regular motel and eat out, but if you are based in one place for a while, say while house-hunting, and would like something a little more like a flat this may be for you.

WHERE TO LIVE

The USA is continental in size. Prices and standards vary accordingly, especially for housing. The most expensive places are in the major cities, such as Georgetown (in Washington DC) or in fashionable suburbs (such as Montgomery County, Maryland, just outside the capital). As in Britain the cheaper areas tend to be far out in the countryside, or in the less than fashionable parts of the city, which can include some adjacent suburban areas (such as the older built-up areas of Prince George's County also just outside Washington DC). The same housing can be ten times as expensive in a booming, fashionable area than in a declining industrial town.

Even within a metropolis, such as Washington DC, you will not know where to find a good place to live without help, a lot of money, or a willingness to make awful mistakes, the latter being a 'learning experience' only single young people should undertake. The social geography of the American conurbation is also constantly changing as areas are gentrified, as racial lines of demarcation shift, and as subway lines are opened. Of course, like most Americans, you might hope a low area you buy into will rise, to your advantage, but it's a major risk even for those well tuned into the city. For a newcomer it's a lottery chance.

But a home in a certain area will not only influence your settling down as a family. It will also influence your standing with colleagues and those you meet, almost like an accent in Britain. Getting housing right is not only one of the most crucial decision to be made but also one that needs to be sorted out quite quickly if motel fees are not to erode your savings when you first arrive.

Rental sector
This is far larger and more varied than in Britain. Though buying is seen as much the same kind of profitable investment as in Britain many people do not wish to be tied down by being responsible for property upkeep. Many people move from job to job and prefer to rent locally,

moving by rental van in an almost semi-nomadic way. Many more developers build for rent, though many have sold out to sitting tenants as city councils enact rent control and tenancy security legislation.

How to find rented accommodation:

- via specialist, fee-paying agencies
- estate agents (*realtors*)
- small ads in the local newspaper
- driving around likely areas and calling in at the rental office within each rental development.

Before you start out on your trek you need to know the lingo which can be quite tricky:

- Flats are deemed **bachelor, studio** or **efficiency** when small and single-room (plus bathroom and kitchen).
- A **walk-up** is something like a bed-sitter in a block without a lift.
- **Cold-water apartments** are precisely that − you need to install your own water heater (though normally big city blocks have traditionally had hot water provided by the landlord rather than the tenant).

Unless you are single or moving in with friends you will probably not want to move into the subdivided, older and larger houses in the poorer neighbourhoods, nor would you want to become involved with **urban homesteading** unless you are already a master craftsman and could transform an abandoned property bought from the city for $1.

If you move into a post-1945 development the chances are you will have access to a couple of communal facilities:

- **Laundry-room,** with huge commercial wash and dry machines for renters' use only − take a pile of 25c pieces. Costs are pretty good, and the time (especially the dryers) is much lower than domestic equivalents.
- **Pool,** available for key-holders and guests. In heat waves this can be a great boon.

Houses may also be available for rent, much more easily than in Britain. These are often available through real estate agents for set periods.

Condominiums

During the 1970s the rental market changed quite markedly. Many developers decided to get out of the rental market, often by way of selling to other developers who wanted to re-develop blocks even though they might be full of sitting tenants. Many blocks were re-developed at great cost, which turned out to be a back-door way of raising the rent legally. Hence such re-development became a way to get sitting tenants out of potentially prime sites.

City councils initially liked the improvement to the housing stock. Too late it became evident that the poor, and then the lower reaches of middle class, were being priced out of their own flats, with the pool of accommodation they could afford declining.

This introduced a new verb into American English: **to condo.** Apartment blocks were transformed into **condominiums** (quickly shortened to **condos** which does not have a prophylactic connotation to Americans as is possible to the British!).

In effect condos are now little more than blocks of individually owned flats, the only trace elements of communal ownership being communal party rooms and sports facilities (plus the pool and laundry room).

Buying

Mortgages are often **fixed rate** rather than flexible as in Britain. This is good news for those buying when rates are low, so protecting the purchaser from further rate rises. For those having to buy, though, when the rates are high a slump in interest rates is of no immediate benefit. Many house buyers attempt to overcome this by refinancing their loan at the new lower rate.

Savings and loan associations are similar to building societies. Once upon a time they only gave mortgages to certain racial and ethnic groups, but since the US authorities stepped in during the 1960s civil rights campaigns this has supposedly ceased. Mortgages today are supposed to be available on the basis of being able to repay the loan plus interest along with the collateral value of the property.

What needs to be done?

- Buy a good local guide to property purchase and property financing. Ask at a public library for a recommendation.
- Get good local legal advice *before* committing yourself to purchasing.

Rates are set locally. In the days before the community charge or poll tax was mooted in Britain the assessment for local taxation in the two countries was very similar, though in the USA rates are called what they actually are: **property taxes.** If you should consider a mobile home check as to how it will be taxed, whether as fixed property or as a vehicle.

Housing types

Being continental in size and variety US housing is more varied than outsiders often realise. The first surprise may well be the widespread use of **wood.** Timber-built houses (increasingly popular in Britain due to price advantages) are often called **frame houses,** though they often have wooden walls too, and in some areas even wooden 'tiles' called **shingles.**

Terraced houses (here called **row houses**) are less widespread in US cities. Baltimore, however, is actually famous precisely for its row houses, unfortunately often covered now with 'Baltimore stone' (pseudo-stone cladding). Many industrial towns of the Appalachian coalfields have town houses perched on hill-slopes much like in the Rhondda Valley in Britain, though wood rather than brick or stone is likely to predominate. Immigrant areas of the eastern cities had vast areas of tenements, many stories high, now often abandoned as urban decay eats out the heart of the once industrial and trading cities.

Far more than in Britain the middle-class and much of the working-class ('blue collar') housing is detached, free-standing in its own lot. In older, generally midwestern or eastern cities, houses are often more European-like, with fairly small rooms. Out west, however, rooms tend to be larger, and many lower middle-class 1940s-50s housing seem very like the farms the owners had left back on the Great Plains of the 1930s Dust Bowl days, like farmhouses without farms, all packed together, yet each on its own plot of land. As the middle classes have moved on to new property such areas have been bought by minorities so that often very poor ghetto areas appear, at least superficially, middle- class to European eyes.

The figure below gives an idea of average house prices in four major cities by relating them to multiples of annual income. For instance, average house prices in New York and Los Angeles are both about $130,000, representing 3.3 years of average annual income, in Chicago the average price is around $90,000 or 2.4 years' annual income, whilst in Indianapolis the average price is around $60,000 or 2.1 years of the local average income.

Average house prices and incomes in four US cities

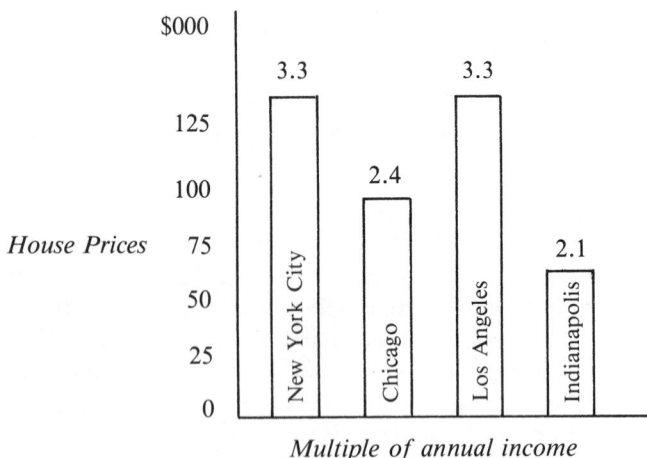

Multiple of annual income

Source: *The Financial Times,* 30th May 1987.

Utilities

Utilities, especially **electricity, gas** and **hot water,** may or may not be included in any rental prices. Traditionally all utilities except the phone were included in the rental paid. As these costs rose (especially for central heating and air conditioning after the oil price rise of the early 1970s) many became separate items. If charged directly by the utility companies bills are usually monthly, with the sanction of being cut-off if you don't pay (or your cheque bounces).

> **Beware:** being paid every two weeks but being billed every month can get you as out of phase as being paid monthly but having quarterly bills to meet in Britain.

The **telephone** is worth an early mention here, if only because recent changes have complicated a system once fairly easy to use and understand for domestic users. The Bell system has been broken up into regional companies with rival long distance carriers, making long distance, especially across country, calls quite complicated and expensive. The domestic rental often includes local calls with long distance calls being separately itemised (a good idea). But even in off-peak hours long distance calls, especially those just outside the local area, are quite costly (like Washington DC to Baltimore, which though a shorter distance than Manchester to Birmingham is deemed long distance at a rate that makes the two cities seem to be in a different countries). This only becomes a real problem when trying to use a call box and being asked for $5 worth of 25c pieces before the operator will connect you. Domestic telephone users should watch out for special deals on long distance calls that may be advertised by your companies. They often have loss-leader rates (to encourage you to get used to using them for long distance calls). For more details see pp.51-54 later on.

For further advice
For general points to consider when moving abroad to live see Michael Furrell's 1986 Daily Telegraph Guide *Living and Retiring Abroad,* published in London by Kogan Page at £6.95. It also has a small section on the situation in the USA.

More detailed considerations are raised in David Hoppitt's *Overseas Property Guide: The Do's and Don'ts of Buying a Home Abroad,* published by Telegraph Publications of London in 1986. Though the specifically US material is rather thin and only relates to Florida and California, the general issues raised are important and need to be dealt with wherever property is bought. These include when to obtain professional advice, ground rules for property purchase, time-sharing opportunities and pitfalls, with details on the legalities of purchase and the securing of the necessary financial backing.

FOOD AND DRINK

Eating out
Fast-food from recognisable companies is readily available, often with extras such as gravy and mashed potatoes or a scone-like piece of bread reflecting local taste. **All-day breakfast** or **salad bars** may well be part of the war between competing hamburger outlets. Breakfast is probably the best bargain, though all-you-can-eat meals at any time of day are good value (though to be avoided if you are on a diet).

For city restaurants you can find any style and pay any price you like, though in country areas steak may be all that is available.

What sort of weekly budget?

- Indulgent: £200 per head
- Average: £150 per head
- Budget: £70 per head

But it all depends upon where you are: rural hitchhikers can survive on breakfast plus roadside fruit stands.

Eating in

Supermarkets vary, but chains are usually excellent for price and exotic choice, including delicatessen items, alcoholic drinks (if locally permitted) and serve-yourself salad bars. Food is priced at familiar European levels, with steak generally cheaper, but with lamb more expensive (and usually frozen from New Zealand). More details on shopping including shopping for food, are given below on pp.46-50.

Incidentals

Drinking in **cafes** and **bars** can be uncomfortably expensive. A cup of coffee can easily cost over a pound. Prices in **diners** and **coffee-shops** (especially in drug stores) can be very reasonable, often with free coffee refills (if you like it weak). **Cocktails** (where alcohol is permitted) can cost from £1.50 to £4, though half that in the late afternoon – early evening **happy hour.** Cigarettes may cost 80p for 20, though prices vary greatly to reflect States' individual tax rates, and all prices are rising with regular federal tax increases ('hikes').

Tipping

The British have a usually well-earned reputation for being mean tippers, especially in the USA. Americans tend to be seen over here as over-generous. In the USA tipping is much more important than in Britain. Those in the food and drink business are usually very underpaid. In fact they usually rely upon tips to survive. As a general rule be generous for good service.

You'll have to use your judgement over how much to leave. Taxi drivers are notorious for their contempt of those who leave less than 10%. About 15% is probably right for bar staff and those serving food. In bars you'll often get a bill each round, though if you become known you'll be able to run up a **tab** to make one payment when you leave. If you pay for each round and leave only the exact money you will probably get ever poorer service. Watch what others are doing. If in doubt ask your friends.

If you are paying by credit card you may notice that when the slip is presented to you, you find the total amount left blank. You are being invited to add something extra for a tip. If you've left a tip at the table make sure you don't end up paying twice.

Alcohol

The story of alcohol in the USA is the story of these United States in all their variety. Over the years America has been a refuge for those fleeing from the gin-sodden old world to a new world of freedom and temperance, and for those who arrived expecting the freedom to do, to eat, and especially to drink, whatever and whenever they liked. These two traditions have fought over and over again, and after the US Constitution had been amended (1919) to outlaw the sale, manufacture and distribution of alcohol it seemed that finally the blue meanies had won out over the boozers.

The rise of the prohibition era gangsters soon turned public opinion, and as part of Franklin D. Roosevelt's New Deal the US Constitution was re-amended in the mid-1930s to allow things to return to what they had been before. This still enabled local communities to rule whether alcohol should be available in their particular locality. College towns are often 'dry', though the first place over the county or even State line may well have bars, liquor stores and little else. In the Appalachian mountains it is possible if lost to tell whether you are in a Tennessee county (wet) or North Carolina county (dry) by looking out for a petrol station − if they hang out a beer sign you're still in Tennessee!

No State still remains completely 'dry', though if several adjacent counties are it may start to feel that way. But even in Mormon Utah liquor stores exist, and you can drink with your meal, though you may have to bring the vodka in with you and get a 'set-up' − a Bloody Mary with everything except the vodka, which you add to taste.

As a response to the rising tide of alcohol-related road fatalities, especially involving teenagers, the general trend is to raise the age of drinking to 21, which makes drinking in a college town very inconvenient. Colleges rarely if ever allow alcohol to be sold on campus anyway (the British student union bar is unknown), *but* you'll need proof of your being over 21, hence the cry of 'you got ID?' You can be 40 and bald and still not get a drink if you haven't got an ID and the barman takes a dislike to your face (or accent).

Bars and pubs

Bars, pubs and other dives may be disappointing. They are often little more than drinking places, with perhaps picking up the same/opposite sex as the only added attraction. Even bars which may be recommended to you may well turn out to be ill-lit, long, thin and uninviting. Beer on draught plus cheap drinks during the late afternoon happy hour with a chance to meet friends after work may be their only extenuating features. Bars often do reasonable snacks, steak sandwiches and the like, plus Irish coffee. Have no faith in the kitchens.

Pubs are bars with the word 'Pub' written outside. They *may* have imported, even European, beers, but at best only Watneys and Guinness. Other beers, though with exotic names, are usually US versions (like so much 'foreign' beer in Britain).

Places you could safely eat in, apart from the expensive bars in the

equally expensive hotels, without fear for your health are likely to be
dry, like the Crystal Palace in Disneyworld. Seaworld does, however,
serve draught beer to those also eating.

A favourite watering hole on Connecticut Avenue in Washington
DC used to have a rat come strolling through from time to time.
Several months later the place was bolted and barred: 'The public
health department finally caught up with them?' 'Hell no, he
didn't pay his taxes!'

Restaurants
Which leads to **restaurants.** Family ones rarely allow alcohol of any
kind. Though this will hardly inconvenience those going in for the all-
you-can-eat breakfast, at the other end of the day after a long time on
the road it may come as something of a disappointment to leave your
motel room for the restaurant over the way, order steaks, and then find
you can order neither beer nor wine (though on your travels you could
yesterday and will tomorrow).

Many communities consider that if you must have alcohol you should
buy it elsewhere, and drink it only in the privacy of your own room away
from God-fearing folk and their innocent children. As you watch people
gorging themselves, blowing smoke everywhere as they eat, and down-
ing Coke like there's no tomorrow you may feel somewhat annoyed
about not being able to get a glass of beer. But tomorrow night in
another town the waitress will appear and ask 'Anything from the bar?'
and you'll know that you've crossed an important line somewhere out
back on the road.

Posher restaurants almost always serve, or permit, alcohol. Presumably such places are deemed for 'grown-ups', who are beyond redemp-
tion.

If in doubt ask people you are visiting what the situation is locally.
Even dry areas have people who want to drink and these people know
all the dodges. They'll know where the nearest available wet jurisdiction
is, and where you can take a bottle to drink with a meal without hassle.
They may well stock-up themselves once a month when going into the
city or over the line, and have a fridge-full ready to be shared with
visitors.

ENTERTAINMENT

As disposable incomes are generally high, Americans spend a lot on going out. The rich love to sponsor and to be seen at cultural events so world class **orchestras**, **opera** and **ballet companies** are found in most major cities, though tickets may be hard to come by.

Rock concerts abound, and you may well be able to see not only US groups but major British ones in those huge sports stadia that all cities and most college towns have. Bluegrass, blues, country, folk and jazz festivals abound, often outdoors in summer. They are generally excellent, and not over-expensive for the experience they provide. As gatherings dear to so many Americans they are worth visiting, if only for their colour, food and drink.

Theatre is still mostly associated with Broadway in New York City, or in the regional theatres that take travelling productions. Some cities have stock (repertory) companies which are often enthusiastically supported locally.

Tickets may generally seem expensive, especially in large cities. Bookings are conveniently made in person at *Ticketron* (see the phone book for location and details).

Cinemas are generally either for films on general release (about $5), or for old classic re-runs (about $3). New York City and Los Angeles have tomorrow's films today, to test audience reaction (at least $10). Smoking is generally banned in all cinemas, there are no on-screen commercials, and audiences can be very raucous. In summer the air-conditioning can be fierce, so take a sweater.

Museums and **galleries** are usually free, though may cost a pound or so. As in Britain specific exhibitions can be rather expensive extras. Beware though the federal budget cutbacks have ended most evening openings of publicly funded institutions, such as Washington DC's Smithsonian Institute (including the Air and Space Museum).

Concerts and the **theatre** can cost at least £10, at least twice that for Broadway hits on the New York stage.

Entertainment parks vary enormously, from £10 (Dollywood in the Great Smokies of eastern Tennessee) to £20 in Disneyworld (though if part of a package holiday Disney may be much cheaper and being prepaid seem an almost painless cost).

DRESS SENSE

It is tempting to view the USA as a more relaxed, unfussy country as far as what to wear goes. The national costume seems to be the T-shirt, jeans and trainers. Such generalisations, however, can be confusingly misleading. There are dress codes (a phrase you may never even have heard before arriving in the US). They just aren't the same as elsewhere.

In New England, those States between New York and the Canadian Maritimes, people tend to be more formal, even stuffy, than you'll find elsewhere. Though casual wear may be okay for the garden or the beach visiting a restaurant casually dressed would raise many an eyebrow, and in expensive restaurants service would be refused. For work most men wear suits and short neat hair. Women do not generally wear trousers ('pants'). But the suits may turn out to be yellow plaid, if not at work then at church socials or town meetings. Casual dress is more acceptable out west, especially in California, in all but the most expensive places.

However, don't be lulled into believing anything goes. Topless bathing hasn't as a rule arrived, even in areas climatically appropriate. There are militant nudists and naturist bathing areas, but nowhere is nudity as casual as, say, on a summer's day in Danish parks and beaches or around the pools in the south of France. That isn't to say there won't be a lot of exhibitionism on beaches, but the rules will be known by all, and if you cross the line you'll soon find out. Watching what others are doing remains a good rule of thumb.

SHOPPING

Shopping centres
In the late 1960s and early 1970s going from Britain to the USA was perhaps most dramatic in the contrast between how and where people shopped. The rise of huge British out-of-town shopping centres, hypermarkets and covered precincts may have reduced the contrast somewhat by the end of the 1980s.

Learn from others' mistakes: don't let your first bag of US groceries melt into a useless mass before you even get it home!
- Frozen foods must go straight home by car.
- If you must go shopping on foot do it as late as possible in the summer, and always keep out of the sun.
- Don't expect shopping to be just like at home only on a bigger scale.

Today the differences for the middle classes are not so noticeable. Tescos, Normid, Sainsbury's, Gateway and Safeway have covered Britain with stores, almost, though not quite, like US supermarkets. But whereas in Britain the out-of-town centres (such as Metro Centre in Tyne and Wear) are the exception (and still newsworthy) thousands of such suburban shopping malls exist across the USA. By 1976 Washington DC had about 12 that made a claim to be malls, half a dozen of which were modern and purpose built.

And as such out-of-town shopping proliferated the downtown department stores dramatically declined, squeezed between suburban discounts (boxed hi-fi at cut prices but with no after-sales service) and specialist shops built into malls (on the main axis between two rival supermarkets). The expansion of jobs out in the suburbs took many commuters away from the central business district, and the impoverished inner city population couldn't support the same level of retail sales. The downtown seemed doomed.

But the 1980s has seen a rejuvenation of many downtown centres (Boston and Baltimore are two of the most well known). Department stores have been revitalised, speciality shops have been reopened, and conferences, tourists and yuppies have moved in. Even so though the downtown shopping will never dominate the whole metropolis as it once did. Rather, downtown will be just one of many shopping opportunities for the well-healed and mobile middle class.

The USA is abroad

Remember this and you'll not expect things to be quite the same as at home, and so it won't throw you off quite so much when things turn out differently from what you expected. If you are used to a range of small family businesses and shops in a town centre you may find shopping in the USA very strange. If you are already familiar with the fortnightly stock-up trips to your local hypermarket after work you'll hardly notice the difference, except for the wider range of goods.

Opening hours tend to be longer than even the most 'open' of British supermarkets, 24 hours a day 7 days a week being not uncommon in large cities (though rare in small towns). Shopping hours in downtown department stores are more likely to be nearer to those in Britain, closing time being about 6 pm, though even here a late night opening may be available. Malls tend to close about 10 pm, with their department stores remaining open 9 am to 9 pm. 10 pm is common time for supermarkets to close.

Blue Laws

Just as Sunday opening is a mess in the UK so in the USA local options determine Sunday opening. Blue Laws are those laws restricting Sunday opening, not the selling of pornography. Generally Sunday opening hours tend to be more limited than other days of the week, and liquor may be on the shelves, but only for sale at certain times (like Good Friday in England and Wales).

Drugstores

These are more than chemists, though not so unusual for those who have watched British chemists diversify over the years. Stationery, hardware, some clothes, certain foods, perhaps liquor and usually snacks with soft drinks are generally available. Look for the green cross for the pharmacy section (or the Mercurial twisted snake symbol, also in green).

Buying clothes and shoes

The good news:

- Most clothing, especially where cotton-based, is usually cheaper than in Britain. It may not be American any more (though if it is, a 'union-made' label may tell you so, as on Oshkosh children's clothes)

The bad news:

- Ignore descriptive sizes. Is 'large' used in comparison to 'small' and 'medium', or 'extra-large' and 'jumbo'? Who knows!?
- Women's sizes appear to be but aren't the same as in Britain. A UK 12 is a US 10, and 10 an 8, and so on.
- For footwear it's the other way around, a British 9 being a US 10 (or perhaps more like a $10\frac{1}{2}$).

More bad news:

- Average width is often the only shoe fitting available.
- Expect poor standards of service in shoe shops and shoe departments of large stores. If you are used to the trained personal service of British shoe shops you are in for a disappointment. The immediate sale is what's important, not cultivating a regular clientele.

Any ways around this?

- If you like fashionable shoes and can jam your feet into average widths shoe shopping won't be too bad.
- If you can get away with wearing work boots these are often excellent value (and often imported from Eastern Europe!). US-made cowboy boots are magnificent and with good care can last for years, if not decades. After fifteen years the author's first pair still go back for resoling.
- Many Americans side-step the problem by using **mail order.** There are specialist firms who meet this problem by offering an excellent service, at a cost, through the post.

- Keep your eyes peeled for shoes available through factory outlets by the side of motorways. These can turn up in the most out of the way places (like firework stores in southern States).

Mail order

Sears Roebuck of Chicago produce what is probably the most well-known catalogue (nearly ¼ million items). Since rural free delivery was introduced by the US Post Office in 1892 urban suppliers have been able to provide, if not the very latest, at least modern fashion and consumer goods to anyone anywhere. As people moved off the land and into the suburbs they kept their faith in the mail order catalogues. This means that mail order firms generally cater for a more up-market, even specialist, clientele than in Britain. Mail order firms deal directly with customers not via an agent (whose commission would either put up prices or eat away profits). Unlike in Britain mail order is not payment by instalment, but by money order (or today increasingly by charge card over the phone).

Specialised mail order is more developed than in Britain, though if you regularly use garden equipment and supplies catalogues or buy outdoor casual clothes (as from Rohan) you will already be familiar with the general standards and procedures. Specialist catalogues tend to be more exotic than in Britain, and include in many States firearms (or 'sporting goods' as they are often called) as if they were little more than fishing rods and trainers!

Shopping for food

Most urban people buy their produce from the fruit and vegetable sections of their local supermarket. The quality is debatable. Certainly fruit is huge and piled high, and is available all year independent of the passing of the seasons. Whether forced giant strawberries, though, have any flavour is hotly argued. Word has it that square strawberries are being grown for ease of shipment! And when you get it all home, wash it to get the chemicals off. Some fruits even have a wax covering that needs to be removed.

The good news:

- Many cities have **roadside fruit and vegetable stalls** along the highways in the surrounding counties. Peaches, for instance, can be bought in season very cheaply from these roadside stalls, and it's very common to stop off and load up on the way back home from a weekend away.
- Many cities have **farmers' markets** downtown in a Covent Garden-like hall. Fresh food is brought in from local farms and is often

excellent and reasonably priced. Food stalls at such markets can be a great treat – everything from pizzas to oysters (in Baltimore at least, with draught beer too!). Taxi drivers, government employees, policemen and visitors will all nip in for a bite to eat, so the quality tends to be fairly good, with prices reasonable. Towns such as Knoxville, Tennessee, that are trying to redevelop a decaying downtown are encouraging farmers' markets adjacent to downtown malls and theatres as a way of retaining, or attracting back, a sense of activity downtown, so quality is encouraged.

More bad news?
- The US is based upon the fruits of mutual distrust. You will often see the sign 'If you broke it you just bought it', hardly the most welcoming of approaches to a casual shopper.
- Record and book stores often will not let you take any bags into their shops, for fear of shoplifting. Don't take it too personally: they distrust everyone. Security will take the offending bag at the door, usually in exchange for a token.

Mutual distrust seems to lead naturally enough to lawyers and doctors. As a rule of thumb:

Get good insurance cover
Keep your head down
and
Get a good lawyer!

LAWYERS AND LEGAL FEES

The US seems to be a society held together by litigation – commerce by other means? The roots of this may well be in the written nature of the Constitution, or conversely the need to regularise relationships in those areas not adequately policed by the Constitution. This is, after all, a free trade economy operating under the rules of *laissez-faire* capitalism. The US is overtly and militantly a property-owning democracy. A major role for contract law seems almost inevitable.

US lawyers generally work on a contingent fee basis ('no win no fee'). This remains illegal in Britain for historical reasons justified today on the fear that it would encourage lawyers to win at any price (else they don't get paid), with a concern not for the case *per se* but for the fee. The advantage the Americans would point out is that in the USA poor people can afford to take large corporations to law knowing that if they lose they will not be stuck with fees to pay. If they win they pay their lawyers a percentage of the awarded damages.

Unfortunately this often leads to lawyers going for vast sums, playing on widespread dislike of large corporations, such as insurance companies, to boost their take. The result is that insurance premiums, for instance, have skyrocketed, and may now be so high that certain groups can now no longer obtain cover. Commerce by other means indeed! But 'payment by results' is deeply ingrained in the American system. Watch *LA Law* on the TV for a view of what this can entail. If you do hire a lawyer on a non-contingency basis expect enormous fees.

As a tourist or medium stay visitor the only rule of thumb is probably to make sure that you carry adequate insurance: health, car and uninsured driver (where you insure yourself against being hit by someone you might have to sue but who hasn't any money or any cover of their own).

HEALTH CARE

US doctors are world famous. Given the amount of debt incurred to get a medical degree high fees are only to be expected. The doctors' 'plight' is helped by the fact that when we are ill everything gets focused upon getting better, so we are vulnerable in the market place — we'll pay what it takes, and doctors know that. To exacerbate the situation most medical fees are paid by the insurance company, so the sick are even less price sensitive. Add to this the doctors' fear of being sued for failure to diagnose correctly something nasty and you have a mass of tests that are deemed standard, are expensive, and anyway the insurance companies will pay up, so what the heck.

To cover themselves most doctors pay about £30,000 in malpractice and accident insurance premiums each year — and that's *before* any costs! So health care is expensive. Getting the prescription filled of course costs extra too!

And get your teeth fixed *before* you go to the USA. There can be no more infuriating experience than being sat in a dentist's chair, cotton wool and sucking tubes stuffed into your mouth, a mean drill burring its way into your teeth, with the costs rising like a taximeter, having to listen to your dentist explain his investment portfolio, all of which involves money he's currently extracting from you.

THE US TELEPHONE SYSTEM

The popular view abroad is that the US phone system is the best in the world, being the cheapest and the most efficient. Many Americans might have agreed with you before the break-up of the Bell System. Today the system is more complex and opinions remains divided as to its efficiency and cheapness. Certainly Americans use the phone at least twice as much as the British. Economies of scale should pay dividends for both users and the phone companies. In the big cities such as Washington DC the system is generally very good for the casual user. Most phones are push-button, directory enquiries are computerised, and most phones can do tricks that have only recently appeared in Britain, such as transferring calls when you are out.

Tones
As soon as you pick up the phone you should hear a constant buzz (unless it's a payphone). The ringing tone is long with long pauses. A short bleep means the number is engaged: you got the 'busy signal'.

Numbers
All numbers fall into a standard system unlike in Britain: typically (987) 654 3210, where the numbers in brackets are the area code and the first three digits the exchange. You may be surprised to find that US phones still have letters along with numbers. Sometimes numbers are given in an appropriate word form: (800) USA-RAIL for the public railroad Amtrack. Be careful not to confuse the number 0 (zero) with the letter O which is the same as the number 6.

The other symbols * and # which are only just appearing on British phones are only involved if you want to programme your phone to do things like transfer calls to other numbers. The only trick you'll find useful is to push the # at the end of punching in an international number (it means: that's it, go ahead and call this number).

The main problem for travellers comes from using public phones for calling outside the immediate local area. Local calls are easy. Just dial the last 7 numbers. Unfortunately not all calls within the same area code are deemed local. Calls outside the immediate vicinity are called 'long distance' even if you don't consider the distance to be very far. You need to place a 1 in front of the seven numbers as in 1-654 3210. For long distance calls with a different area code (as would always be the case if calling another State, and might be the case within a large State such as New York or California) use a 1 followed by the area code plus the seven digit number, as in 1-(987) 654 3210.

Charges
Most calls except from hotel or motel rooms are comparatively cheap, especially within the local area. Long distance calls from private phones are itemised on the next bill so you can pay back friends precisely what you owe them. Cheap rates apply from 5 pm to 11 pm Sunday through to Friday, with bargain rates from 11 pm to 8 am daily, all day Saturday

and 8 am to 5 pm Sundays. Use a private phone where possible as it's considerably cheaper than from pay phones.

Public telephones
You may have difficulty finding these in certain areas, such as many residential neighbourhoods. Try anywhere people congregate (launderette, gas station, 7-11 store, etc). Post offices do not generally have telephones as in much of Europe.

Usually you'll need a fist if not a bag full of loose change. You have to put in the minimum fee (which varies from 10c to 25c) just to start the process. If you end up reaching an engaged number you'll get your coins back. The money gets you the dial tone and a local call, still of unlimited duration in some areas. Even to call the operator on a free number ('toll free') you'll need to start the process off with the minimum fee, which you'll get back.

If you dial a long distance number a voice will cut in to tell you how much more to put into the machine. As the largest coin is 25c you'll need lots of these handy, and your call will be for a 3 minute minimum whether or not you want three minutes. Where you get hold of $2.75 in quarters in the middle of nowhere at three in the morning to call ahead and warn your hosts that you've had a flat tyre is not the company's problem. They probably can't understand why you aren't calling 'collect'. You may end up having to hope your friends will accept the call.

If you have an account with a US phone company you can use special phone boxes that take credit cards, but these are usually only available in large airports. Calls based upon price rather than time are rarely available, and again usually only from major airports.

Calling home
The international prefix is 011, which should be followed by the UK code (44), then the British area code minus the initial 0, followed by the number. A call home then might be 011-44-(782) 621111. For international information call **1-800-874 4000**, a free service (as are all 800 calls). As local operators in rural areas may not be able to help you place a call home from a public or motel phone (they may never have been asked for this service before, or if they have you may not be able to understand what they say) this number can be very useful. Telephone boxes rarely if ever have the kind of information about making calls that is normal back home, and telephone books probably won't help either.

How much does it cost? The standard rate from New York City to Britain applies from 7 am to 1 pm local time. The discount rate is from 1 pm to 6 pm and the super discount is from 6 pm to 7 am A one minute call dialled direct from a private phone during the cheapest period costs about $1.50, with additional minutes at half price. The minimum three minute call from a pay phone would be about $6.50.

Some useful numbers
- Local directory enquiries   411
- Non-local directory enquiries with the same area code   1-55 1212
- Directory enquiries for numbers with other area codes   1-111-555 1212
- To find an area code   411
- Operator   0
- Emergency services   911
- Wrong number dialled   211
- Toll-free numbers directory   1-800-555 1212

WHAT TO READ ON THE USA

There are plenty of general books on the USA. Visit your local public library and you'll find anything from a row to a room full of books on various aspects of US history, geography, politics, literature, economics and travel. But more up-to-date information for the traveller has to be sought elsewhere. The larger the bookshop the larger the choice of up-to-date guidebooks. Large city shops such as Dillon's in central London or Blackwell's in Oxford may well have a whole wall just on the Americas (North and South) plus as many more on general travel hints.

The vast influx of British visitors to the USA that grew when the pound was considerably higher than today stimulated a new wave of articles in papers such as the *Daily Mail, The Guardian, The Financial Times,* and *The Observer.* Keep an eye open for their travel pages for up-to-date information (though beware: some articles result from trips paid for by specific sponsors who may well have set a schedule to make the most of their good points). However, more reliable information can be found in *Travel Which?,* back numbers of which are available in your local public library.

Guidebooks in general
In trying to decide which guidebook is for you remember:
- Practical information varies in degrees of detail. Guidebooks are most likely to be useful for background information on history, food and the popular sights. If using their practical travelling details check the date of publication as important details can vary substantially from year to year. This is particularly so for library copies, which are usually older editions than in the bookshops. Certain

guides are updated each and every year, and usually make this a selling point.

- Accommodation lists can be detailed and thoroughly inspected, the personal choice of the author, or the result of users' anecdotal reports (unchecked by anyone). You have to check how and when any guidebook is compiled.

- The degree of detail varies considerably and deliberately. There are generally four types of guide:

1. **General Travel** – may be a guide to travelling in general throughout the world, where the USA section is small, possibly superficial and only one of many country-by-country offerings, and so is inadequate for any serious traveller. On the plus side they may have information applicable everywhere including the USA if interpreted intelligently. A good example would be Ingrid Cranfield's *The Traveller's Handbook,* published since 1980 by Heinemann, or more specifically Maggie and Gemma Moss, *Handbook for Women Travellers,* published by Piatkus in London 1987 (£4.95).

2. **USA-at-large sightseeing guides** are useful for general essays on regions like the South, the West Coast, and so forth, plus general essays on US society, history, geography and climate. A typical example would be *Fodor's USA 1987* guide, regularly updated (also available in parts for various regions and cities).

3. **Budget guides** are geared mainly to young people on tight budgets, but their up-to-date practical hints, phone numbers, recommendations and warnings can be invaluable for all visitors. An example would be *Rough Guides.*

4. **Pocket guides** are just that, but they can be very useful, especially if dealing with a specific region or city. *Berlitz* guides are the best example here. Beware, though, that some pocket guides assume you are six feet tall with large anorak pockets, not 5′4″ with only the pocket in the back of your shorts.

Specific guidebooks

Here are some of the major guides you are likely to find readily available:

- **AA guides** are more usually associated with European countries, but are increasingly available for such US cities as San Francisco. These are a revival of the definitive Baedeker nineteenth-century guides. The AA partnership seems to be producing increasingly modern, readable and useful guides. Their layout is very attractive, with good photographs, helpful hints for seeing the sights, how to use public transport plus general history and geography of the city.

Copies are paperback, but in plastic covers (with a useful pull-out city map). They are not cheap, and may be too detailed for a quick visit. Updating is not annual, so beware. Coverage of more US cities, though, would be very useful.

- **Berlitz Travel Guides** are cheap and cheerful, attractive to read, authoritative and carefully compiled. Some are updated each year. They are truly pocket guides, and the Florida volume in particular is good value. The colour maps are a bit garish, but nonetheless useful. Cost: about £3 each.

- **Fodor Guides** offer lots of practical information whether on the whole of the USA or on specific regions. They are, however, dull collections of facts, though being regularly updated they offer a vital measure of assistance when arriving in a strange city on a country-wide tour. The Washington DC volume is quite useful. The *Fodor Budget Guide* to US cities is an abbreviated version of the national volume with some useful hints for budget travellers. Fodor also provide guides for adjacent areas – Canada, Latin America and the Caribbean. A newly commissioned series is expected soon.

- **Michelin Green Guides** are for those with larger pockets (as in Rohan bags). They cover regions and specific cities, the former for touring by car with an emphasis on historical sights, monuments and famous vistas. The city volumes are excellent, with clear maps, well translated text (from French originals), and they are particularly recommended for excursion suggestions, with consideration given for stays of various lengths. The New York City volume is excellent, with subway maps, bus routes and tours laid out, and includes covering material on the various neighbourhoods.

- **Rough Guides** are, as their name suggests, aimed specifically at budget travellers, particularly the young (and young at heart). They tend to be more upbeat, and give the reader the feeling that the writer has actually enjoyed visiting the place in question. Practical facts are available, as well as historical and cultural information. All visitors may enjoy their concern for off-the-tourist-trail places to visit and things to do. The New York City edition is particularly interesting. Their strong points are that they are contemporary, well researched and at a reasonable price. However, they have a distinctly budget feel about them, compared, say, to the glossy Berlitz guides, which may put off some people.

Finally there is a long-standing personal favourite:

- **Traveller's Survival Kit – USA and Canada** which is specifically geared towards young people, especially students able to spend at least a long summer in North America. Compiled by Susan Griffin and Simon Calder for Vacation Work of 9 Park End Street, Oxford, the 1987 edition costs £6. There are sections on red tape, currency, health insurance, getting about, where to stay, living it up, and where to find the best buys. This book has been updated over the years, having its origins in the British Universities North America Club (BUNAC) guides of the late 1960s and early 1970s. It is a wealth of things to do and to avoid, plus phone numbers. It is a great Linus blanket if you ever get into a fix. A similar volume available within the USA is *Let's Go USA 1987* by Harvard Student Agencies.

What's suitable?

If you are spending some considerable time in one place, like New York City, you may find it worthwhile first checking out the range of books available from libraries. The larger the library the larger (and newer) the selection. Then visit a large bookshop if at all possible and browse for as long as you can. You'll need to ask yourself:

- *How long in any one place?* If only a few days are involved, say in Florida, a pocket Berlitz will probably be enough. A week or more and a Fodor-like guidebook would be an investment.

- *Is the guide for the car, a coat pocket, or for shorts?* The large Fodor volumes are heavy and are definitely for the car. A Berlitz though would fit into a shirt pocket.

- *How accurate and up to date must the information be for me?* If you are on a pre-paid tour by coach or even in conjunction with a particular motel chain you won't need vast amounts of budget accommodation information, so a borrowed copy giving general sights to see should be enough if you check your copy's date of publication, and make any necessary adjustment for inflation. If in doubt, ring ahead to the resort or attraction for current prices.

Longer stays

As you read such material you will come to realise that most of it refers to being on holiday, whether from a US or a UK base. People do of course spend up to several years on working holidays and these guides can be invaluable. But by and large these books don't cater for long-stay visitors' particular problems. *The Traveller's Survival Kit — USA and Canada* has enough information for the long summer vacation tourist to be of some use for the long-stay resident, but for people actually living in the USA with their families a new type of guide is needed. Only gradually is this guide for living in the US appearing. You are reading one now!

For interest try also Roger W Hicks and Frances Schultz, *Long Stays in America,* published by David & Charles, Newton Abbot, 1986. Despite an excellent cover the text's layout manages to hide a lot of excellent material. This is a book to read rather than to use as a reference source. Don't be put off by the poor quality and the irrelevance of the illustrations.

Maps
These are not generally available for the USA, except those suitable for the motorist. Town plans in guides are often of little use except in the most general sense (to show the relative locations of the sights). Fortunately most US downtowns, but not all, are on a regular grid system so sketch maps of US inner cities are of more use than equivalents for European cities. Better town plans can be obtained locally.

For those drivers who don't want to rely upon being able to pick up highway maps at petrol stations (and gone are the days when they were both plentiful and free!) the Rand McNally *Road Atlas* is now available in UK bookshops at about £6, and it covers every state and most cities. It is a wonderful book go delve into, to work out new routes, or just to reminisce. It is very widely available throughout the USA – where you will probably find a cheaper and newer edition.

For details as to how to find local maps see Victor Selwyn's *Plan Your Route* published by David & Charles of Newton Abbot in 1987. See particularly Chapter 7 on the maps of the southwestern deserts.

US equivalents to the Ordnance Survey are not widely available to the general public, except in US Parks Service bookshops within National Parks. Topographical maps by the US Geological Survey are excellent if you can find them. US colleges usually stock their local maps, as may their bookshops.

In the UK probably the most comprehensive collection of USGS maps is held by the University of Keele, Keele, Staffordshire ((0782) 621111, extension 3554, Mr Keith Mason, curator), which can be viewed by appointment for purposes of research.

Other viewpoints
People from overseas have visited the USA since its founding and have written many guides for explorers, travellers, visitors, emigrants or just the readers back home.

- Probably the most famous within the USA remains *The Domestic Manners of the Americans* by Mrs Frances Trollope, mother of the *Barchester Chronicles* author Anthony Trollope. Her comments

from the 1830s are often unintentionally witty as she surveys the rise
of the common man, slavery, utopian experiments and the new
cities. Americans hated her. Mark Twain said it was because she'd
hit the nail on the head. Later Charles Dickens did the grand tour,
recording his impressions in *American Notes*, recently republished
by Penguin in paperback. His novel *Martin Chuzzlewit* is also based
upon much of this first hand experience.

- Recent views are numerous, and many are well worth reading.
  Jonathan Raban has canoed the Mississippi for his *Old Glory*, a
  Picador paperback. Other academics have used the novel to explore
  the excitement and trauma of being a Brit in the USA. Malcolm
  Bradbury (of *History Man* fame) wrote *Stepping Westward*, an
  Arena paperback which both confirms and confounds the *Dallas*
  glamour image of the West. Later David Lodge explored the late
  1960s California through the eyes of an initially staid Birmingham
  university teacher in *Changing Places*, a Penguin paperback. If you
  don't manage to read these before you visit the USA you must do so
  upon your return!

Americans on themselves

But what of Americans' *own* views of themselves? The list is endless.
After all, most of what has ever been written in English has been written
in the USA. The size and ethnic variety of the USA mean it is impossible really to read about America at large, except that many American
writers were often engaged in satirising the narrowness and provin-
cialism they sensed all about them at home.

The nineteenth century saw such great writers as Walt Whitman,
whose *Leaves of Grass* has a freedom of line and a delight in the
vernacular sounds of everyday life that exalts the promise of everything
democratic while coming to terms with the reality of the Civil War
slaughter. If ever visiting the battlefields read Whitman's elegies for the
fallen (which of course came to include President Lincoln in 'When
lilacs last in the doorway bloomed...'). Mark Twain too explored the
quality of US society and what it was to be American (a still popular
theme). His classics include the documentary *Life on the Mississippi*,

from which emerged his masterpiece *Huckleberry Finn* where a white child and a black slave together learn more about the ways of the world than they would wish to know, and in so doing throw into relief both America's promise and failings.

This sense that the US was finding it impossible to mature with honour recurs in F Scott Fitzgerald's *The Great Gatsby* where the romantic view of American promise is shown to have been plundered by the rich, who, by the 1920s, have turned the US into little more than just another country, no worse and certainly little better than elsewhere.

The Great Depression of the 1930s confirmed this for many Americans at large. John Steinbeck explored the fate of many ordinary working people in those harsh times in *Of Mice and Men* (1937) and especially *The Grapes of Wrath* (1939), an epic struggle of the newly landless to survive the Dust Bowl of Oklahoma and their crushing disillusionment with the Promised Land of California. Both the book and the subsequent film (with Henry Fonda) remain classics.

This theme also affected much popular music. Woody Guthrie's *Dust Bowl Ballads* are still heard in the music of Bob Dylan and Ry Cooder in the 1970s and 80s.

Since the 1940s American writing has expanded beyond all bounds. Richard Wright's *Native Son* and Ralph Ellison's *Invisible Man* have opened up the black experience to an ever wider audience, though possibly the most eye-opening account remains Alex Haley's *The Autobiography of Malcolm X*, the posthumous story of the slain radical (available in Penguin paperback). Evan Hunter's *Streets of Gold*, a Corgi paperback, explores the New York immigrant experience more realistically though perhaps less commercially successful than Mario Puzo's *Godfather*, a Pan paperback.

This leads into mention of the movies, for *Godfather II* is one of the most accessible explorations of New York immigrant life on the big screen.

But New York City has been seen in many lights. All offer a glimpse that can lift the visitor into a world of both imagination and concrete reality: *The French Connection* (1971); *The Taking of Pelham 123* (1974); *Marathon Man* (1976); and *Midnight Cowboy* (1969). Even the *Stepford Wives* (1975) explores one threatening image of the suburbs as seen by the big city enthusiast. *Three Days of the Condor* (1975) is very strong on downtown Manhattan and Washington Heights, though it is possibly television's *Cagney and Lacey* or *Hill Street Blues* that explore what many see as being the actual and threatening reality of New York City. Movie buffs can compare these television interpretations with the movies *Fort Apache the Bronx* (1981) and *Assault on Precinct 13* (1976) (though the latter is actually set in Los Angeles).

Learning about the USA

For those wanting a more structured and academically based introduction to the USA there are courses available both here and in the USA.

- Courses on a wide range of topics are put on by the American Studies Resource Centre. Enquiries can be made via:
  Josephine Woods
  Short Course Unit
  The Polytechnic of Central London
  35 Marylebone Road
  LONDON NW1 5LS
  (01) 486 5811

  If you contact the Adult and Continuing Education Centre at your local university or polytechnic they may well have short courses on topics such as American Film, Presidential Elections or American Literature.

- The National Federation of Women's Institutes has put on such courses as *Mississippi: Great River of the World; New York City: World City;* and *The Wild West: Fact and Fiction* at its own residential college in the Oxfordshire countryside. Contact your local WI secretary for details of the college programme, or write directly to:
  The Principal
  Denman College
  Marcham
  ABINGDON
  Oxon OX13 6NW
  (0865) 391219/391425

- For courses in the USA contact the Cultural Attaché at the US Embassy or write directly to:
  The Institute of American Studies
  State University College of Arts and Science
  Potsdam
  NEW YORK 13676
  USA

  whose courses on the US media, US politics, US history, US art, US folklore and music are 'for educators, university students, business people and other professionals'. Courses are described as being an 'immersion program' and cost about $1,000 for a month plus about $200 a week accommodation (and you have to get there).

- You could go the whole hog and take a degree in American (meaning US) Studies. The major teaching departments are at the universities of Sussex, East Anglia, Manchester and Keele. A well used route is to take American Studies as one half of a joint honours programme. At Keele for instance American Studies can be studied alongside:

> Biochemistry, Computer Science, Electronics, English, Geography, Geology, German, Greek, History, Law, Music, Philosophy, Politics, Russian and Sociology as a 4-year programme.

As a 3-year programme American Studies combines with:

> English, Geography, German, Greek, History, Law, Philosophy, Politics, Russian and Sociology.

For further details contact:
> The Senior Tutor
> University of Keele
> KEELE
> Staffordshire ST5 5BG

So what else can I read?

Books on the USA can and do fill libraries. Useful readable introductions to its history, geography and economy are less easily found at reasonable prices. A general introduction to the contemporary USA can be found in David Stuart Ryan's *America: A Guide to the Experience*, published by Kozmik Press, London, 1986, at £9.95 in paperback.

US history books tend to be huge, heavy and expensive. Recently a couple of reasonably priced paperbacks have appeared and are recommended: Peter N Carroll and David W Noble, *The Free and the Unfree*, Penguin, Harmondsworth, 1977 (about £4), and Hugh Brogan, *The Pelican History of the United States of America*, Penguin, Harmondsworth, 1986 (about £6). In hardback the latter is a bookclub selection too.

Contemporary issues are explored in a recent Macmillan paperback series edited by Christopher Brookeman and William Issel of the Polytechnic of Central London's American Studies Resource Centre. Titles include: Christopher Brookeman's own *American Culture and Society Since the 1930s*, William Issel's *Social Change in the United States 1945-1983* and Sam Rosenberg's *American Economic Development Since 1945*. For readers interested in the how and why of urban growth since the last war try Kenneth Fox's *Metropolitan America: Urban Life in the United States, 1945-1980* in the same series published by Macmillan, Basingstoke, 1985-6.

But for a practical guide to places of historical interest try *An Historical Guide to the US* published by Norton in 1980 for the American Association for State and Local History, price £22.

4
Preparations at Home

Paperwork done in good time can make all the difference when going abroad. But besides everything involved in getting entry into the USA you also need to make certain arrangements at home:

- selling or leasing your home, or terminating the lease
- storing or transporting household effects
- getting yourself and your family over to the USA (see Chapter 6)
- sorting out any tax implications of changing countries (Chapter 9)

THE HOUSE

If you are leaving for a sufficiently long time, if not quite for good, you may need to consider selling your existing house. As your major capital asset you will probably need to sell in order to buy another in the USA. The Consumers' Association's self-help guide may be helpful in this.

With estate agents, solicitors and surveyors offering ever more comprehensive services selling is not quite the hassle it once was. As you are not simultaneously a buyer you are not so deeply enmeshed in the chain of buyers and sellers that bedevils so many. This should make your property quite attractive to certain people, such as first-time buyers who are not themselves part of any chain.

Certain fundamental questions need discussing though:

Should we keep the house rather than sell?
If you intend to return to the UK it may make a lot of sense not to sell but to lease the property while away. Then there's somewhere to live upon returning.

BUT – if you need the equity tied up in your house you'll probably have to sell. If this is so, remember that when you do at last return house prices will in all probability have risen a good deal, so you'll need to return from the USA with much more than you left with, just to stay even, never mind better off.

Should we lease the house?
If you can afford to leave your equity intact then do so, but leaving it unoccupied can be a recipe for disaster

- your mortgage still has to be paid
- your insurance is usually based on the assumption that the house is generally occupied
- it may become a target for thieves and vandals
- you'll find the garden very overgrown, and yourself very unpopular with neighbours if you haven't made adequate arrangements for the grass be be cut, and leaves swept and so forth.

Unless you are going away for only a few months do not leave it unoccupied. Even if you are only away for the summer it is still highly vulnerable so:

- cancel the milk, papers, coal, etc, and get a neighbour to push mail and circulars completely through the letter box.
- arrange for the garden to be kept neat and tidy
- if possible arrange for a housesitter. A student relative writing a thesis might love the peace and quiet in exchange for mowing the lawn (and feeding the cat!). Or maybe friends would like to stay for a couple of weeks while you're away, using it as a holiday base?
- join an exchange system: vetted foreign visitor uses your home and car while you use theirs. Details from:

> International Home Exchange Service
> 6 Siddals Lane
> Derby DE3 2DY
> (Derby 558931)

How do we lease our house?
If you are going on a staff exchange a simple house plus car swap may be possible, to everyone's advantage and convenience. Even if you aren't going on an exchange you may be able to contact someone who is coming to Britain much as you are going to the USA. Academic staff from the USA often stay at UK universities over the summer or when on a term's leave and require suitable accommodation while the pursue their research — check with the notice board of local universities' senior common room (SCR), staff house or equivalent staff room.

Ensure your building society will let you lease out your house. If you explain the situation in good time, particularly if it is for a set period, they may well be agreeable.

Use a reputable agent, or rent via a reputable college. Accommodation is always needed by colleges, but you'd need to enquire as to what controls, if any, the college would exercise on its students living in your house. Contacting someone who has rented via the college may help to ally (or confirm) your fears.

Any snags in leasing out our home?
Assuming your building society raises no insurmountable objections you need to consider:

- Will the rent cover the mortgage plus reasonable wear and tear?
  If you don't know — get out the calculator and work it out!

- Will the tax office continue to accept that it is a principal dwelling house, and so eligible for continuing tax benefits?
  Talk to your local tax office.

- How do we account for the rent as income for tax purposes?
  Again you need to talk to your tax office.

- What possessions to leave out and what to store?
  If you are exchanging with known people you may feel it necessary only to empty wardrobes, storing what you are not taking with you in the attic in labelled boxes. If you are letting on the open market you will probably want to put into storage a lot more, such as your collection of jazz records and the hi-fi itself. It might be worth storing such items elsewhere, such as in the in-laws' attic. However, the more your stuff is left in the house the more self-evidently it remains your house and home. This may be important when you return and seek repossession.

- How will be obtain repossession upon our return? What if we return early?
  A good agent may be able to help here. Getting tenants out of accommodation, even furnished accommodation, can be time consuming, though if it is quite obvious that you are returning to live rather than to sell with vacant possession this can usually be managed without too much of a problem, particularly if it is explained to would-be tenants *before* they settle in.

A few further considerations
- Don't be tempted to put everything in storage, rent as unfurnished, and then expect to move back in at a moment's notice. Rent controls and security of tenure legislation will make repossession against a tenant's wishes very difficult, expensive and troublesome. It may be possible to arrange a licence rather than a lease if you feel unfurnished is necessary. Set a definite date for your return to repossess and the licence should, if done correctly, enable you to

exclude the tenancy from the terms of the Rent Act. You will probably need expert advice from a solicitor who deals particularly in housing law to get this right.

• Remember that you don't know your tenants as well as you might think even if you know them at all. Even family friends will now have children who may have perfected the art of wear and tear. For some families dirty shoes aren't allowed beyond the front step; for others dirty feet on sofas go quite unnoticed!

• A general book that may nevertheless help the expatriate is Robert B Davies's *A Layman's Guide to Profitable Letting*, published by Jofleur of Watlington (Oxfordshire) in 1986.

SHIPPING POSSESSIONS TO THE USA

Travelling to the USA may turn out to be the easiest aspect of the whole saga, once the paperwork has been completed. At least you are unlikely to lose anyone *en route*. Moving your possessions can be quite another thing, and a hassle-free move will require careful preparation and a certain amount of luck. Certain questions need to be asked:

Who is paying to ship everything over?
• Your new employers?
  If so, they may have a preferred carrier. Check before committing yourself elsewhere.

• Yourselves?
  Check the rates very carefully. What minimum load is involved? If 200 kg is the minimum might it not be cheaper to prune things down to an absolute minimum and take them on the plane with you rather than involve a different carrier? And who is going to pay to bring your things back at the end of your contract, when the exchange is over, or just when you decide America's not for you?

How bulky or how heavy?
• Check with the various carriers carefully. Bulky items in non-standard shapes may well incur penalty charges with one firm, whereas the weight may be more crucial with another.

• What's included in the price? Is insurance? Is packing? What about door-to-door service? These items cannot be too carefully checked and cross-checked. Even then you may get an inconvenient surprise once you arrive if nothing shows up.

An anecdote of warning!

A metal trunk (US=footlocker) was packed with college papers and summer clothes, sealed with the required US Customs declarations and the keys were given to the shipper as instructed, some six weeks before required for the August 24th start of the new term at the University of Maryland. Six weeks later nothing had arrived at the other end, even though the agreement was door- to-door for a specific date.

On contacting the shipper it turned out that the trunk would be awaiting collection at College Park railway station. This, it turned out, no longer existed. Then the shipper said it was still on the docks at Liverpool, but should arrive for collection at the docks in Baltimore (30 miles to the north) within the month.

Six weeks later the US Customs issued a notification to collect or be charged $5 a day from Dulles International Airport in Virginia (30 miles in the other direction). The paperwork had gone astray so the trunk had to be claimed and taken through customs in person, during office hours. The loan of an estate wagon made this possible. Their invoice said the trunk came via Canada and New York by land and sea, but in fact it was stored with other items that had just been flown in from London Heathrow.

Five years later the same footlocker was booked in as excess luggage on the trip back to Heathrow, but on arrival at Heathrow it turned out still to be in Dulles awaiting the next day's flight, necessitating a further trip to the airport. Even the best laid schemes...

Excess baggage is one way to take necessary goods with you: 28 kg per person (if length + depth + breadth aren't greater than 157cm) generally goes free with the APEX fare across the North Atlantic (though this may be liable to a charge on cheaper flights to Newark). Anything over 28 kg goes at the excess rate, which can be very expensive if charged by weight rather than by piece. It may be possible to send extra baggage by a cheaper freight rate if booked beforehand.

What should I leave behind?

Remember all those holidays where you came back with half the clothes unworn, half the cassettes unplayed, and half the toys unused? This time you have no room for anything that isn't absolutely necessary.

- Most British electrical goods are useless on the US 110V (60 Hz) supply. Even a 240/110V converter will mean the motor speed will be of no use for tape decks and record players. Whereas immigrants to New Zealand may find it worthwhile to ship out household goods like dishwasher, due to electrical compatibility and the high local prices, this is not so for the USA where goods are generally cheaper and need no adaptation for US-sized rooms.

- Furniture is cheap and readily available for the newcomer in the USA. Garage sales are a usual way for all sorts of people to sell off excellent furniture at rock bottom prices to avoid the shipping costs within the USA before they move. British arrivals will be amazed at what's on offer, or what may even be given to you by people glad to be able both to help out and to clear their own garage of spare beds, sofas and so forth.

  Of course shipping out fine furniture is another matter, whether it is antique or modern: if you can afford to ship it you'll be the envy of your colleagues. However, beware: the humidity range is quite unlike that in Britain, which may affect fine furniture considerably. Expert advice on preservation is as worthwhile as advice on shipping.

What should I take then?

During the Second World War the slogan was 'Is your journey really necessary?' Something along these lines needs to be asked, and you need to limit yourself to items that are:

> very special,
> very useful, or
> very personal.

- *Personal effects:* from ornaments to books via records to jewellery. If you don't expect to return, or at least not for several years, you'll probably want your favourite Beatles EPs, your photographic albums, and your wedding souvenirs. If your stay isn't too long these could all go into storage.

- *Household goods:* though most US accommodation comes with cooker and refrigerator buying all new kitchenware, pillowcases and duvets (even where available) can be very expensive, even if you become a great garage sale devotee. Don't bother with the garlic press you've never used, though your Edwardian parsley-cutter may be decorative enough to take along for display in your new kitchen.

- *Clothing:* a great opportunity to leave most of what fills your drawers and attic to your local Oxfam. You might like to fit yourselves out with new shoes before you go. Many Britons seem to prefer Clarks shoes to what's available over there.

Even if you leave all your furniture and concentrate upon lesser chattels it is quite likely you'll still end up with 500 kg per grown up. That's half a tonne each! If you intend to take books this figure will be easily reached. If your library is an essential part of your professional tool kit you may need to negotiate a special arrangement with your new employer to ship them *en masse*. Fortunately the US mail permits books (as educational material) to be shipped overseas very cheaply — if sent by the mailbag load to a single address. So the return move, even if at your own expense, isn't so expensive.

What should we put into storage?
Find out how much it costs to store and insure (and who provides the packing cases and the shipment to the place of storage). If the cost of storage is greater than the replacement value you alone can decide whether or not the sentimental value is worth this extra expense. Most people returning to their stored possessions find that too much rather than too little has been retained, so storage preparation is a great opportunity for a mammoth clear-out. 'Triage' is the name of the game: three piles, one for essentials to keep, one of things to be disposed of, and a third pile for the rest. The hardnosed would say store only the one pile of essentials! Get rid of the rest: chairs you know you'll never get around to repairing, flared jeans, and old school textbooks.

If your new employer offers to shift all your goods and effects rather than pay for a preset amount it might be worthwhile shipping everything over and putting the whole lot into storage over there while you look for somewhere to live. Self-storage lock-ups are now quite common in the USA. A row of miniature 'garages' will be enclosed in a compound, with a resident guard, so things should be quite secure. If you must leave valuables, such as antiques, in such a depot don't advertise or talk about the fact. Any security can be broken if the price is right!

CUSTOMS AND EXCISE

UK
Private household goods can usually be exported from Britain without too much hassle. Export licences will normally be granted for privately owned, albeit valuable, items if they are not being taken abroad for sale.

- If you have any doubts talk to your shipping agent and make enquiries from your local office of Customs and Excise (which are not based just around the coast or even just at large airports).
- For their address see the telephone book.

US

Customs will allow in bona fide household goods, clothes and personal effects. Though a container-load of micro chips will not be let in despite your hobby as a hacker, a load of obviously household and family goods will, if you can show the necessary papers to support your arriving with the kitchen sink. Do not arrive with all your worldly goods and a tourist visa (unless you can get everything into two suitcases).

- It may help US Customs and yourself if you list everything as you pack it (it helps if a box does go astray to know what to claim for). Any item could be taxed on its value, so you need to estimate some figures, though you can guess some, such as 'Sports gear $50'.
- To get a sense of what is necessary ask the Customs Desk at the US Embassy ((01) 499 9000) for their free sample inventory list and information package.

Remember: Meeting and dealing with incoming families and their belongings is hardly something new for US Customs, so they'll know both what they want and what they want you to do to make your arrival easy (if only for their convenience).

5
Visas and Immigration

These States are the amplest poem,
Here is not merely a nation but a teeming
Nation of nations.

Walt Whitman.

A SOCIETY OF IMMIGRANTS

The USA is not like the Old World, a place of permanence and continuity, adapting only so far as it preserves what has been. The USA continually reinvents itself, turning 'them' into 'us'. It is a nation that does not grow from affinity with the soil or even with one language whose origins are lost in time. Instead the USA is polygot, an ingathering of all the races, peoples and religions of the earth. It has always relied upon attracting people from elsewhere. Even the native peoples (mistakenly taken for 'Indians') came from Siberia in the dim and distant past.

Europeans came initially to dominate the modern influx, but just as the British came by the turn of this century to be outnumbered by peoples from eastern and southern Europe, so too this once novel combination has recently been overtaken by a continuing influx from Latin America, south-east Asia, and even from Africa. The dominant black and white mix has recently given way to browns and yellows.

Twenty-five years ago most immigrants came from Europe or from Canada. By the mid 80s most are Mexicans, Filipinos, Vietnamese, Koreans, Indians, Chinese and Jamaicans. They arrive on jumbo jets; they walk across the border; they are washed ashore on the Florida Keys. A flickering fear says aliens are overrunning the country. If the USA is a lifeboat in a world of trouble maybe it is in danger of being swamped. Racism re-emerges, fuelled by fears of recession-led competition for jobs. The long-standing mutual fears and suspicions of blacks and whites give way to mutual apprehension that those browns and

71

yellows recently let in will throw open the gates to one and all, levelling down, with English but one of many possible tongues.

But this has always been the fear. Benjamin Franklin feared that the Pennsylvania of the 1750s would be overrun by Germans. In the 1840s the Irish seemed about to swamp the towns and, while digging the canals, the countryside too. Later Jews, fleeing Czarist hostility, brought their Yiddish language, their Hebrew writing, and their Saturday Sabbath into the growing cities which many Americans feared were being turned into foreign countries. Working for the good of their children, immigrants stood together when necessary and plunged into the mainstream when possible, learning English, voting, investing their lives in almost any job that would keep the family intact.

John F Kennedy, son of an Irish family made good in the USA, saw his country as 'a society of immigrants, each of whom had begun life anew, on an equal footing'. For him America's secret was that it was 'a nation of people with the fresh memory of old traditions who dared to explore new frontiers'. It was in his memory that the USA abandoned the old 1920s quota system which, if too late to keep the USA White Anglo-Saxon and Protestant (WASP), at least had kept it predominantly European. Since 1965 new waves of immigration have brought newcomers not just from Europe but increasingly from the Third World. Of the 544,000 legal immigrants in 1984 the largest number came from Mexico (57,000), the Philippines (42,000) and Vietnam (37,000). Britain came ninth (only 14,000).

For British settlers (or even visitors) recognition of this change is essential. The British have a very ambivalent attitude towards the USA. The temptation is to see it as a richer, larger version of the south of England with more snow and more sun, but still recognisably British (if not quite English). If this were ever true the mass influx from southern and eastern Europe of Italians, Yugoslavs, Jews and Poles last century has long since swept over this British heritage. The countryside is full of people originally from Scandinavia and Germany, as the place- names of the Midwest tell us (see Harrison Keillor's *Lake Wobegone Days*, Penguin 1986, for a loving but caustic look at such people in Minnesota). Today's Third World influx is changing the very language and landscape of America. Where once there were small ethnic enclaves like San Francisco's Chinatown, now there are vast Spanish-speaking neighbourhoods in most cities. The mayor of New York City may be from a Jewish background, but elsewhere mayors are likely to have been born in the Philippines or in Cuba. In Delaware the Lieutenant Governor was born in China. In 1984 the Immigration and Naturalization Service (INS) caught 1,3000,000 illegal immigrants. The US Census Bureau reckons they missed between two and three times more. Most are from

Mexico, crossing the land border in a dash from the conditions of
Bangladesh to those of West Germany in one night. No wonder that the
INS requires visitors to provide proof they intend to leave. A cynic
might say that the less the INS can control the 2,000 mile land border to
the south the more it needs to demonstrate its authority where it can
with those coming openly into the USA at airports.

BEING AN IMMIGRANT: SETTLING IN

The USA has always offered immigrants a prize: land, a job, or freedom
of expression. But it has rarely been an easy bargain. The streets have
never been paved with gold. Those who expect gold have been severely
disappointed. Just being alive is a risk. We are all immigrants in the
sense that we are all travelling into an unknown. To go to the USA is to
compound that. You are going into someone else's future, which you
must make your own. The familiarities of home, relatives, bank holidays, the passage of the seasons, cup finals, TV programmes, *The
Archers* or *Desert Island Discs* will all vanish to be replaced by the
occasional long-distance telephone call, harsher seasons (or no seasons
at all), cable-TV with 36 channels spouting religions and languages you
don't recognise, not to mention more advertisements than you thought
possible. From all this novelty you'll have to carve out a new routine, a
new set of familiar surroundings which you'll have to be prepared to
jettison at a moments notice when promotion means leaving Portland,
Maine, for Portland, Oregon. And you may see the children even less
than before.

Arriving in the USA it may be tempting to see yourself as remaining
essentially who you have always been, though with more money as
befits being within a wealthier economy. Feeling like this many immigrants have been very bewildered when they were asked to change their
lives again and again. The company may be taken over and all existing

staff fired. The department of history may be closed as a university cost-cutting device. The union may call you out on strike, and you lose.

Such traumas are of course increasingly likely back home. Indeed changes such as these may be what encouraged you to leave for the USA! But the price of that extra pay, the extra promotion prospects, the better funded library or laboratory may be the greater risk. If your company gains a Star Wars military contract you will have to go along with that or leave with no other job in sight. Being offered promotion may be on the 'up or out' principle (take it or leave the company) which may leave you in a part of the USA you'd never intended to visit never mind settle in.

Great courage and flexibility will be needed in this kind of situation. If you really do want to stay in the city where you've started to settle down, greater flexibility in job selection than you've ever had before may be necessary. Teachers drive cabs, act as tour guides, write free-lance, work for political candidates in the hope that their election will lead to a job in their office.

As there is less of a safety net in the USA, networks of friends and family take on ever more importance, and hard work and commitment are essential, with an enthusiastic endorsement of the US's 'can do' attitude, rather than the more pessimistic 'what if it doesn't work out?' US attitudes to success and failure, while rewarding success more, also encourage risk and so don't take failure to be a mortal sin. It is not a sin to be knocked down. It is only a sin to stay down. By having taken the leap of faith necessary to become an immigrant you are already making a stake in becoming American, and may find flexibility more appealing and less threatening.

All members of the family should have talked the options and implications over though. If after staying for a year in one place a move seems imminent it will again need to be talked through, and if all were aware early on that this might happen the house can be treated like a long-lease summer cottage and all the further packing, saying goodbye, changing schools and so on can be seen as a further adventure so that the family can stay together rather than as a rude awakening.

VISAS

US citizens easily enter the UK on a valid passport, some travellers' cheques and a return ticket. Despite attempts to give reciprocal rights of entry to the USA this has not happened yet: entry visas are still required until 1989.

There is a bewildering variety of visas, and the appropriate regulations can and do change at any time without notice (though any major change would get considerable publicity). Visas are broadly:

- **non-immigrant** for those intending to return home at some date, and
- **immigrant** for those wishing to settle permanently.

In practice however there are intermediate statuses, some of which can be changed, and some which cannot. So it's essential to know what status you want, and what the limits and potentials are of the status with which you enter the USA.

How do I know which visa I need?

The non-immigrant or immigrant distinction seems pretty straightforward. Unfortunately it isn't always quite so simple:

- Going for a look around prior to applying for a job?

You'd probably do best to go in on a tourist (non-immigrant) visa. But if you do apply for a tourist visa don't confuse your applications by saying that it's a job-hunting exercise: you may well be refused entry. Enter and leave as a tourist. Then apply for another, more appropriate visa to re-enter.

- Not wanting to commit yourself to settling down but wanting to enter the job market free to change jobs at will?

An immigrant visa is necessary. Visas given for those with specific job contracts stipulate that you must leave if you end your contract with the sponsoring employer. However, once legally inside the US it may well be possible to change your status (say for instance if you've married or have had children while living and working in the USA).

NON-IMMIGRANT VISAS

There are **twelve** types of non-immigrant visas (each with a different letter prefix). All applications must satisfy certain conditions. Applicants must be sound in body and mind, have no drug or dependency problems, with no criminal record (which includes advocating polygamy!), must not be nor have been a communist (or Nazi collaborator!). And of course applicants must not be entering the USA to 'overthrow, by force or violence or other unconstitutional means, the Government of the United States or of all forms of law'. Or as the US guidelines sum up:

> 'In short, aliens who do not measure up to the moral, mental, physical and other standards fixed by law are, with very few exceptions, excludable from admission even if they have the necessary documents.'

> **Important point:** A US visa is *not* permission to enter the USA. It is merely a statement by the US authorities abroad that they know of no reason why the bearer shouldn't be permitted to enter. Admission is actually granted by an Immigration and Naturalization Service Officer at the port of entry. Arriving on a valid tourist visa with all your worldly possessions, all the family (including grandma and the dog) would suggest to the most hardpressed INS officer that you might be entering the USA for more than just a few days at Disneyworld.

The conditions which applicants must satisfy are set out in some detail in the official booklet *United States Immigration Laws: General Information* issued by the INS and available from the US consular authorities (ask for booklet M-50).

Visa types
There are twelve basic types. When applying it is essential you know which category is appropriate or your application will get rejected, which can add to the already lengthy process time that you can ill afford to lose:

- A   diplomats and consular staff with authorised families
- B   visitors for business or pleasure
- C   transit visas
- D   ship and aircrews due to leave soon
- E   businessmen or investors
- F   students to 'pursue a full course of study at an established institute of learning'
- G   diplomatic visas for international organisations
- H   (1) for those of 'distinguished merit and ability'
      (2) temporary contract where a US worker is unavailable
      (3) recognised trainees
- I   bona fide media people
- J   student, specialist or academic to join a recognised programme
- K   fiancé(e) entrance, valid for 90 days only prior to marriage and change to permanent resident status
- L   intracompany transfer

Most visa types permit spouse and children under 21 to go with the applicant, though care needs to be taken as to whether or not they can then work. For instance, the spouse or children of a student (F) visa may not work or even apply for permission to work. Intracompany transfer spouses and children may only work if they've successfully applied for work visas in their own right.

Documents needed to support an application depend upon the visa type sought, and whether or not the issuing official suspects fraud. Proof of intent to return home is necessary. But how can anyone prove intent? Well of course you can't, but you can provide evidence that returning home is more important than staying on in the USA:

- the need to return to complete a degree or to further a career:
  - a statement from your college saying you must be back by a specific date or forfeit your place
  - a statement from your company setting a date by which you must return or forfeit promotion
- a return ticket (rather than just money or a credit card) suggests an intent to return home by a specific date (say 12 months for an APEX ticket).

The more footloose and fancy-free you appear to be to the US authorities the more necessary it is to show you have a compelling reason to return home.

Someone with a mortgage, children in school, an established career and a return ticket plus a package tour to Disneyworld is less likely to be asked for further proof of intent to return than a recently graduated single male with no return ticket, or a single female with child care qualifications and a single ticket to a wealthy suburb (who would appear to the suspicious INS as a potential and illegal nanny).

A sample application
Let's try for a tourist (B-2) visa. What's needed is:

- a full British passport valid for 6 months beyond the intended date of return
- a visa application form (optional form 156)
- a recent photograph ($1\frac{1}{2}$in^2) with your usual signature on the back
- 'evidence substantiating the purpose of your trip and your intention to depart from the United States after a temporary visit.' Optional form 156 suggests how to deal with this requirement.

Speeding up the process:

- Ring (01) 499 5521 for current information.
- Ask for a form by ringing (01) 449 7895.
- All applications must now be by post. Be prepared to wait a month or so, especially in early summer.
- There are emergency provisions if you need a visa for an urgent and unexpected trip. Ring (01) 499 3545. You'll need a good reason, like

a funeral, winning a Concorde weekend in New York where the prize must be taken immediately, an intracompany transfer due to an emergency in the US branch, or some such event.

● Put a US visa into your passport if there is any likelihood you may need one in the future. Use a slack period when you don't need your passport, and when you do suddenly need to leave for the USA you'll be ready and able. Of course without an established UK career you may not be granted such an open-ended visa.

This example is of course an application for the most popular visa. For immigrant visas (see next section) the procedure is going to be much more lengthy.

Applicants for A, G, H-2, H-3, most I, and L visas will be handled by someone else, usually an employer (or would-be employer). K applicants of course will have a fiancé(e) to help them with the necessary papers. E and I visas are special cases, dealt with as such, and F and J visas involve the appropriate college providing evidence of status.

If a **visa petition** has been submitted to the INS in the USA to establish a preferential status, say for an immediate relative, the paperwork comes from the overseas applicant's US contacts to the INS for approval. If successful the INS forwards the paperwork directly to the consular office dealing with the applicant overseas. For certain employment visas (H-2, H-3 or L categories) the 'intending employment party' must file, whereas professionals, or 'exceptional ability' status applicants, file with the INS themselves via the local US embassy.

IMMIGRANT VISAS

The great age of mass immigration came to an end in the 1920s following the arrival of an unprecedented number of people from eastern, central and southern Europe. A system was then introduced with high quotas for the countries of northwest Europe, and low quotas elsewhere. In the 1960s this was recognised to be a system inappropriate for a nation attempting to rid itself of the legacy of a deeply racist history. Instead, immigration was ended for everyone, except for those able to present themselves as legitimate exceptions. The guiding principles for being allowed to enter became:

● refugee
● family reunion
● to help the USA (skills, investment, etc).

In theory at least there were no special preferences beyond these humanitarian and self-evidently advantageous ones. Reality, though, is a little more complicated.

Refugees
These have an automatic right of entry. In practice anti- communist refugees (such as Vietnamese boat-people) are welcome (if they have some US link) whereas those from right-wing regimes are not (Haitian boat-people).

Family reunions
These involve 'immediate relatives', that is the children, spouse and parents of US citizens. Children must be under 21 and unmarried. Further details are laid out in the M-50 booklet.

Preference system
Such applicants are those who enter the USA to benefit the US economy within a system devised to allow in family members, other than the immediate family, to join members already in the USA. If this sounds like a pig's ear it is. There is a 'preference category' system, and a non-preferential status, and together they are subject to an upper numerical restriction, about a quarter of a million each year, with no more than 20,000 from any one country. What follows is only an outline, to suggest how complicated the rules become, and why so many people end up using the services of a specialist lawyer.

Preference category system
- *1st preference* (20%): US citizens' children aged 21 or over (ie too old to be included as 'immediate relatives').
- *2nd preference* (26% plus any of 1st preference's 20% not used): Spouse plus unmarried sons or daughters of 'permanent resident aliens', that is children of immigrants who are not yet US citizens.
- *3rd preference* (10%): Professional people or those who 'because of exceptional ability in the sciences or arts will substantially benefit prospectively the national economy, cultural interests, or welfare of the United States and whose services...are sought by an employer in the United States'.
- *4th preference* (10% plus any not used by higher preferences): Married children of US citizens.
- *5th preference* (24% plus any not used from higher preferences): Siblings of US citizens over 21.
- *6th preference* (10% of total): Those capable of performing permanent jobs for which there is a US shortage of employable and willing persons already in the USA. unobtainable in the USA are necessary, usually provided in conjunction with the US Department of Labor.

Non-preference category

This is a 7th preference group in all but name. If the preference applicants have left some spare places then others may apply on a first come first-served basis, but with 'Labor Certification' as for the 6th preference still needed. And the queues are very long. Just occasionally a lull in preference applications leads to an unanticipated opening as in 1986 when 10,000 places became available and were allocated by lottery. People were invited to apply, and the first valid 10,000 were granted visas. This was unusual, and may never happen quite like this again.

Once the visa has been issued you need to use it within 4 months to be admitted for 'permanent residence'. This doesn't mean you can never leave, but that if you do so without having taken out US citizenship you may lose your right of re-entry if you stay abroad too long.

OVERSTAYING

If you overstay for a few weeks it will hardly lead to having the FBI after you, but if you should be unlucky enough to get caught you may find it goes against you should you ever try to return. If you leave by way of Canada there'll be no-one to collect your US Immigration form (you'll probably just get waved through on the US side of the border). If you have overstayed on the US side the Canadian authorities will want to know that you are leaving straightaway: they don't want to be lumbered with you as the US won't take you back. You may, however (if you keep mum), be waved on into Canada and so be able to leave for Britain without trouble (few western countries are interested if you are on the way out).

If you want to stay legally you will need to contact the INS (see the phone book to check their location and times of opening). As they will assume you are trying to stay to work you should take necessary papers with you. The best thing to do if possible is to take a US relative or friend along to vouch that you are staying on for family reasons, have a place to stay, and intend to return home. You'll need to complete the INS form *Application for Issuance or Extension of Permit to Re-enter the USA*. Written proof that you have to be back home to start a job, enter college, or some such would be very useful (as would a return ticket).

If you want to change your status you will need a lawyer. Initially, though, you need to know what a lawyer can and cannot do for you. Read Howard D Deutsch's *Getting Into America: The US Visa and Immigration Handbook,* Hodder & Stoughton, Sevenoaks, 1985 (a Coronet paperback). This has copies of all the forms you'll ever be likely to need to know about, with categories of both immigrant and non-immigrant visas comprehensively explained.

ALIEN REGISTRATION

Every alien 18 years or over is required to carry a **Certificate of Alien Registration** or *Alien Registration Receipt Card*. Being more scared of losing this than of being found without it this author kept his safely at home, carrying only a driving licence locally, and licence plus passport if going further afield. Changes of address must be filed with 10 days, and every year aliens must report their address whether it's changed or not.

All of this is very complicated, seems very organised, but ignores the fact that most illegals enter the US over the Mexican border not on 747s from Europe. But those who wish to be in the system as soon as they arrive had better get used to the idea that the paperwork needs to be done, and done right. Of course if the paperwork is done for you by family, college or employer in the USA it's a very simple system, with perhaps only a single trip to the consulate necessary.

Go to it!

US ATTITUDES TOWARDS IMMIGRATION

Despite a tradition of immigration a 1985 poll found that only 27% of Americans agreed with the idea that 'America should keep its doors open to people who wished to immigrate to the US because that is what our heritage is all about.' Some 67% agreed that 'this philosophy is no longer reasonable, and we should strictly limit the number.' Some 56% said legal immigration is now too high, though 66% still approved of offering sanctuary to those oppressed overseas.

If Americans are uncertain as to how they should respond to continuing immigration how should would-be immigrants respond to the USA? In the past British emigrants have been able to disappear into the White Anglo-Saxon Protestant mainstream. Many adults lose their British accents almost as quickly as they pick up US words and phrases. Children make the transition in weeks. But what if the USA turns out to be something like *Hill Street Blues* rather than *Dallas*? Actually even then the difficulties are not too harsh.

The very rules that require immigrants to be skilled, educated and going to a specific job or family reunion mean that most British people will slot right into workplace and neighbourhood with little more difficulty than if they had merely moved to somewhere at the other end of the UK. In fact, moving to another EEC country might well be more confusing with language and legal systems so different from the US-UK traditions. Some people, however, find a move within Europe less traumatic than one to the USA. Continental countries are so obviously different and foreign, whereas the differences within the USA may only creep up, as when there's an illness, or there's sudden need for assistance and you turn out to be the only person in the car park who can speak English. Of course if you treat the USA as a foreign country, which it is, such problems may seem less bizarre and unexpected when they do occur.

British immigrants will be caught in a cross-fire of US expectations. A British accent means you are stuffy but sophisticated, swinging but old-fashioned, staid but cosmopolitan, and so forth. You'll be expected to play darts, golf and soccer, drink only warm beer, stout or G and Ts, and eat only fish-'n'-chips and roast beef. And of course you'll be pressed to drink tea even if you'd prefer coffee or even a beer! Enjoy it or ignore it. Just don't complain that the water wasn't hot enough in the tea (or that the coffee is very thin by European standards).

As an immigrant you may have to be prepared to be more serious about life than those settled back home can be. But this can make the adrenalin flow, that most American of juices.

For British arrivals, though, experience suggests that the more highly skilled, the more firmly middle-class, the greater the chances both of making good in the USA, and of becoming American. For the USA the immigrants' greatest value is as a leavening agent, yeast to reinvigorate society and the economy. Economically immigrants generate more than they themselves consume. Socially they add variety for which the US is famous, acting as an antidote to the blandness otherwise enveloping much of the USA.

Ironically, most immigrants, or at least their children, seek to merge with the mainstream. And the British arriving as part of the brain drain have not gone into exile in the same way as the Vietnamese, the Cubans, or Soviet Jews. The exiles didn't so much abandon their countries as feel their countries abandoned them. The brain drain scientist can always go home on visits, for funerals and wakes, or even to return. The exile cannot.

Both groups, however, straddle two cultures. They leave behind a train that continues on its way regardless. The Britain they leave will not spin its wheels awaiting their return. Yet the emigrant/immigrant can never become a true American, for that requires more than even citizenship or allegiance to a set of ideas. It requires the experience of growing up in a country, the sense of 'my home town'.

6
Getting to the USA

BY SEA

It used to be fairly straightforward to travel to the USA by sea. This was often cheaper, avoided flying for those who still feared this method of tempting fate, and enabled large amounts of baggage to be taken along at reasonable rates. Containerisation has undermined traditional freight services that provided such passenger accommodation. However, some travel by freight vessels is still possible. Contact:

- Navis, Billhorner Kanalstrasse 69, D-2000 HAMBURG 28 (telephone: 010-49-40-78948 234).

The cargo trip Hamburg to Philadelphia, a two week crossing, would cost about £600 (but of course you'd first have to get you, your family, *and* your stuff across to Hamburg!).

Only if you want a cruise *en route* and they offer you a good baggage rate (so you can take all your boxes in the hold) should you consider going over by transatlantic liner. Some cruise liners bound for the Caribbean do go over to New York City first of all (to pick up the bulk of their passengers) so you might be able to find a place. Certain student families returning home from New York City to Britain have returned on vessels such as the liner *France* just for the baggage allowance (with a glimpse of the high-life thrown in).

BY AIR

The North Atlantic is the most heavily used long-distance route anywhere. So the good news is that there's plenty of flights. The bad news is that the fare structures are very confusing (even for travel agents!).

The main variations are:

- ordinary full price
- advance excursion booking (APEX)

- charter fares
- standby fares
- economy airlines
- 'bucket shop' fares.

Ordinary full-price tickets
These provide great flexibility as any ticket is almost as good as money, being exchangeable with and between airlines. Tickets can be cancelled without penalty, and there's a generous baggage allowance with good service. If your employer will pay for this then well and good.

Who buys ordinary tickets? Those for whom money is no object and where flexibility is essential.

Advance excursion (APEX)
These tickets are the most popular form of advance booking as they have a significant price advantage over full-price fares. Tickets must be bought some three weeks in advance (though sometimes this period is changed to meet market demand). Once into the three weeks period, though, no change of departure or return date is permissible (except at deliberately prohibitive cost). Fortunately single tickets (costing half the return price) are usually available, which is useful if you wish to return from somewhere else or at an unfixed future date.

Who buys APEX? Those needing to trade off price for flexibility, and staying no longer than a year (maximum validity). If you know your dates APEX may well be for you.

Charter fares
These are supposed to be for interest groups booking together, though travel agents have been known to cobble together passengers of no common interest except that of a cheap ticket. There's always the danger of being 'stung' with these pseudo charters, especially given the risk that once you are there your firm may go broke (or hasn't paid its bills) and so your return ticket becomes worthless.

Who's for a charter? Those who can't resist the chance of a bargain, and who will not be too inconvenienced if things go wrong, such as single people. You need to be young enough to sleep on airport floors as the Embassy arranges repatriation!

Standby fares
These are a way of filling those seats still unsold at time of take-off. At certain times of year these are readily available, but at other times you may have to hang around airports for days, hardly possible with a schedule to keep, or with young children along with you.

Who's for standby? Single, young people with flexibility at both ends of the journey.

Economy airlines

These have been instrumental in forcing the larger companies to increase their flexibility, helping make standby fares a normal feature of airports. Though People's Express and Laker have disappeared Virgin Atlantic still provides cheap, no frills, scheduled services. The low prices may mean they are booked up long in advance for the holiday season, though at other times you may be able just to turn up on the day. Airports they use tend to be second rank, Gatwick and Newark rather than Heathrow or JFK.

Who uses them? Low-budget travellers, particularly young people who don't mind a very basic flight.

Bucket shop

Fares of this type are usually more associated with long distance flights to other far flung parts of the world like Hong Kong and Australia but can be found for the USA. Tickets are for regular, scheduled flights. They are cheap full-price tickets, with all the advantages if obtained from a reputable supplier. These specialist shops handle the airline companies' spare seats which are regularly available at certain times of the year to specific destinations. Discounts are up to 50%, the tickets are legal and valid, and the system is supported (if somewhat surreptitiously) by the airline companies.

Beware: It is not unknown for bucket shops to spring up, take deposits, and then to disappear without issuing tickets. Reputable shops use reputable airlines and issue standard format tickets from well-established premises. Don't part with vast sums if you have any doubt about the shop's standing.

Who could make good use of them? If you are too late for APEX tickets and can't face hanging around airports for standby tickets then bucket shops may be able to help, especially for off-season travel (though if it's New York you want standby, or an economy airline should be considered too).

If you only want to see a fleeting glimpse of at most a couple of large US cities there is one further option: as part of a grand tour deluxe:

The round the world option

STA took over NUS student travel in 1976 with their string of agencies on university campuses throughout the country (plus high street outlets in London and Bristol). STA fares generally have no age restriction (unlike the 26 upper limit for cheap rail passes within Europe). Round the world from London is £816 calling at Delhi, Bangkok, Singapore, Sydney, Fiji, Honolulu and Vancouver.

STA Travel:
- 74 Old Brompton Road
  LONDON SW7 3LQ   } (01) 581 1022 for intercontinental
- 117 Euston Road   information
  LONDON NW1 2SX
- 25 Queens Road
  BRISTOL BS8 1QE
  (0272)294399

If you do want to fit the US into an around the world trip the best start may well be with Katie Wood and George MacDonald, *The Round the World Air Guide,* a 1987 Fontana paperback which provides information on all international airports, with advice on planning routes, tickets, stop-overs, and possible hassles. Try also Frank Barrett's *A Consumer's Guide to Air Travel,* a 1986 Telegraph Publication paperback for £3.95.

How to choose which type of ticket
Keep a lookout in the travel pages of the newspapers and watch the travel programmes on television for current changes in practice (like news on stolen tickets flooding the market, a carrier about to go broke, etc).

It also pays to phone around; try these numbers:

- American Airplan   (0932) 24166
- BA Poundstretcher   (0293) 518060
- Intasun   (01) 460 3001
- Jetsave   (0342) 27711
- Pan Am Thriftsave   (0800) 010300 (a free call!)
- TWA Jetways   (01) 637 5444
- Virgin Holidays   (0293) 775511

Consider your family status: are you really willing to take the same risks with others besides yourself as you did when a student? Or do you really want all the frills when a day or so camping out at the airport could leave you enough money to hitch out to the West Coast? Be honest with yourself as to your real needs, discuss it with others, and then make a coolly reasoned decision. How critical would things be if it turns out you made the wrong decision?

Most Europeans bound for the USA fly into eastern airports, though those bound for the west coast can fly direct to Los Angeles, one of the most overcrowded and least pleasant experiences. Travellers from the Far East or Australasia will pass through customs and immigration in Hawaii (an attempt to take the pressure of the facilities in Los Angeles).

NEW YORK CITY

London to New York City must be the world's most competitive international route. Six airlines run scheduled services between **London-Heathrow** and John F. Kennedy (JFK), the major terminus on Long Island: Air India, BA, El Al, Kuwait Airways, Pan Am and TWA . From **Gatwick** British Airways will presumably take over British Caledonian flights to JFK, with Virgin Atlantic and Continental (the latter having taken over People's Express) flying to Newark, New Jersey (just across the Hudson from Manhattan).

Fare structures are complicated as explained above, but (April 1987) range from £320 for a 'bucket shop' deal to over £3,000 for Concorde. If you have the time to wait around BA, Pan Am and TWA offer one-way standby fares from **Heathrow** at about £180. Check out BA's new arrangements from Gatwick. For those with schedules planned well before there are Early Saver returns at £400 (£420 weekends) and £270 one-way Savers (£290 weekends).

Specialist travel agencies worth contacting include:
- Slade Travel ((01) 202 5135): return from £240;
- Trailfinder ((01) 937 6544): return from £250 three times a week (or £280 for seven-day-advance-purchase, three flights a day).

Look in the newspapers for new prices and deals, especially the quality Sunday papers.

Gatwick (very accessible via Victoria Station, through-trains from the Midlands and North via Kensington-Olympia, or the M25) is a good source of cheap fares: Virgin Atlantic starts at £130 one way, call (0293) 38222. Compare this with Continental's daily £240 one-way service to Newark, call (0293) 776464.

Manchester has 4 services a week by BA to New York City (at same prices as from Heathrow).

Weekend breaks
- **Virgin Holidays** ((0293) 775511) has a package of return flights, 3 nights hotel accommodation plus a ticket for a Broadway show: £339.
- **Travelscore** offers 3 nights from £399, 7 nights from £569.

DIY holidays
- **Meegson Services** ((01) 734 7282) can book accommodation at ten New York City hotels from £28 a night.
- **Urban Ventures** ((051) 220 5848) or **Homebase Holidays** ((01) 886 8752) offer bed and breakfast from about £20 a night.

WASHINGTON DC AND BALTIMORE MD

Both BA and Pan Am fly direct to Dulles International Airport in northern Virginia from about £200 one-way standby. Though over 20 miles from the White House, Dulles is served by an excellent limited access expressway straight into the heart of the city, with links to the freeways to Baltimore.

The alternative is TWA into Baltimore-Washington International outside Baltimore on the Washington freeway. It's actually very little further from the White House than Dulles, and for the Maryland suburbs of the capital considerably nearer and more convenient.

A **fly-drive** package via either airport is good value for Washington DC if you want to explore the surrounding countryside (a great delight that's a well-kept secret overseas). BA Poundstretcher APEX fares are from £370, and unlimited mileage for 2 weeks starts at £110. Pre-paid motel accommodation costs about £30 a night

TIPS FOR THE JOURNEY

If you've never flown before here are a couple of essential points to bear in mind:

- It's the safest way to travel.
- Drink only water, juices and soft drinks. Flying such long distances produces dehydration, which alcohol only makes worse. So save the free little bottles of wine and spirits for later – in some motel late at night when you've just pulled in off the freeway you'll really enjoy a well- earned shot of your favourite tipple.

Immigration control
Have your passport ready on the plane (not in your luggage in the hold) for filling in the various official US forms. The immigration form asks for your address (a relic of the view that new arrivals are coming to settle down rather than to travel around as tourists?). Give a friend's address, or a motel address (make one up if necessary, for example the Holiday Inn, Orlando, Florida).

After the immigration official has checked your form it'll be stapled into your passport above your visa. Keep it like that until you are leaving (when an airline representative will take it and return it to the authorities).

Customs

There's no red/green choice, so every arrival meets an officer face to face. Keep your passport ready — if only because customs officials seem less understanding for returning US citizens. Be prepared to open *all* your cases as they check for drugs, weapons and fruit.

You may be required to identify your baggage immediately you clear immigration, but it may then disappear for collection elsewhere. Presumably dogs and X-ray equipment have access to the baggage. The process is particularly evident in large airports, and those with substantial links with Latin America (such as Orlando International Airport next to Disneyworld).

Insurance: property and health

It is necessary to buy cover *before* leaving the UK. It is unlikely to be available in the USA (until you become resident, but that's another matter). Check with your credit or charge card company as to whether or not 'free' cover is available for those using their card for booking the flight and accommodation. If you have an 'all risks' household insurance package you may already have 60 days world-wide cover. Check your policy's small print, and double-check with the agent (and even they may have to check with authorities higher up).

Returning home

Always phone to confirm your return flight at least a couple of days beforehand. Schedules may be changed for all sorts of reasons — air-traffic controllers elsewhere may be on strike, or bad weather may have trapped planes half a world away. Check in in good time, especially if you have lots of luggage and a family. Getting on board in a relaxed frame of mind is always a good idea, especially when planes are likely to be full. Families will want to sit together, and a good seat for the film may save a lot of on-board aggravation from disgruntled offspring for the shattered father or harassed mother.

7
Travelling About

WHY TRAVEL?

The USA is continental in scale. Not to experience this is to miss an essential ingredient of the country (almost like Americans visiting Europe and seeing nothing of its historical traditions). *But*, being so vast, the distances can eat up much of your precious time, whether you are a visitor or a resident. Hence the attraction of flying.

Do not try to see too much, especially in your first trip. Vary your schedule so that though some days may involve 400 miles of freeway others will involve taking detours to visit historical sights (Civil War battlefields or colonial settlements are excellent, and usually inexpensive). Driving the country roads can be very interesting and a great change of pace. Driving from Atlanta to Washington DC? Try US15 across Virginia, or even the Blue Ridge Parkway, both of which run parallel to major freeways.

Don't expect to visit four national parks in four days. Even if you can manage the driving you will probably get scenic overload (as in 'Oh no! Not more mountains' felt towards the end of six weeks criss-crossing of the Rocky Mountains). Would you want to 'do' Snowdonia in one day, the Lake District the next, and then the Highlands before Edinburgh *en route* for London-Heathrow?

TRAVELLING BY CAR

For anything but a coach tour a car really is essential for everyone visiting the USA. Even a one-resort holiday can be greatly improved by a few days visiting nearby sights, theme parks, or just experiencing the open road.

The USA is larger, and the distances between cities greater, so the time needed to explore is that much greater than in the UK. Costs per mile are low compared to Europe, but the distances so great the overall costs can still be quite a surprise. There *are* positive aspects though:

- local car hire is very reasonably priced
- petrol is very cheap by European standards
- motoring means wide roads and lots of places to park
- for most of the freeway network driving is actually relaxing due to the legal 55 mph maximum. (Around cities, though, freeways are like bad sections of the M1.)

So a holiday based, for instance, near central Florida's Disneyworld can be both wide-ranging (Florida Keys to the south, Fort Augustine in the northeast, and Panama City to the northwest) *and* very reasonably priced, especially if car hire is booked as part of the flight and accommodation package, or just pre-booked from UK representatives of Avis or Hertz. Such special rates usually involve collecting and returning the car from the same airport, and may require you to stay within the one State (which may be larger than the UK!).

CAR HIRE

A few numbers to try in the UK *before* booking:

- **Avis:** (01) 848 8765
- **Budget Rent A Car:** (0800) 181 181 (a free call: ask for Budget Plan North America)
- **Hertz:** (021) 643 8991; (061) 437 8321

Questions to ask
- What's the **collision damage waiver** (CDW) and the **passenger accident insurance** (PAI) situation? US booking clerks will assume you know what these terms (or even initials) mean, and may never have had to explain them before. Ensure that *you* know what they mean!

  Without CDW you are liable for collision damage (up to a present figure like $3,000). For peace of mind CDW is probably essential, though costly (an extra that can be up to 30% on top of the quoted or pre-paid costs).

  PAI is more modest, but may be unnecessary if you have already bought adequate health insurance for your trip before leaving the UK. Check your policy's small print for whether you need extra PAI. Don't rely on advice from the sales clerks: they won't know.

- Is the car hire **restricted** to the one State? What about a trip from a Florida base over into Georgia? Is this permitted? Is suitable insurance cover available? At what extra cost?

- Can the **booking** be done **via the airline company** at the time you buy the airline tickets?

- What's the **minimum age** for hiring or driving a hired car? Premiums may be required for under-25 drivers.

- What **size of car** would be suitable? A family driving any distance (Miami to Orlando is a 6 hour drive on the freeways!) should avoid sub-compacts (Austin Metro equivalents) and go for at least a mid-range 4- or 5-door saloon (or least a Ford Tempo) which will have adequate luggage space, a good air conditioning unit, and plenty of inside room. Travelling 55-60 mph on the US motorways may be smooth, but it may also be very boring, so comfort, room to stretch, with a suitably powered engine (less noisy if nothing else) are essential.

Remember: Travelling just around Florida is like travelling up and down the length of Britain in terms of distances. Travelling around the USA is *continental* travel. Would you drive the family from London to Athens in a Fiat Uno or a VW Beetle? If you can, fly. If not, use as large a car as you can afford.

- Can a trip **start** and **end** at **different** places? If so what are the drop-off charges? These can be very steep: sometimes equal to the initial hire charge. But having driven from Miami to New York City who wants to drive back down I95 to avoid a couple of hundred dollars drop-off charge? It may be worth paying the charge to be able to stay and enjoy New York City rather than to end a family holiday with four days driving flat-out on the freeway (plus motel charges that would probably equal the drop-off charge alone).

- Can **all payments** (except petrol of course) be made **before leaving** for the USA? Or will there be extras, such as state tax or deposits on the vehicle? Taking a 'fly-drive' package from a major UK or US airline may mean low or no deposit, minimum hassle, and priority booking (at an advantageous price).

- If your **credit card** is used for ID (identification) will it also be used to **block-off** a line of credit as a **deposit?** This question needs some explaining. Even though you may have pre-paid for your car hire (perhaps as part of a 'fly-drive' package) most hire companies will still require an Access (which they will call Mastercard), VISA or American Express card as ID.

So far so good. But beware: they may well use your card to block-off a credit line of several hundred dollars as a deposit. This is not a credit from your account into theirs, to be recredited upon your returning the car intact. Rather it is blocking off a part of your unused credit line.

For instance, if you have £1,500 as your limit with £500 of outstanding debt, then you have a credit line of £1,000 left. If the car hire company were then to block off £200 for the duration of your hiring their car you would only have £800, not the £1,000 you might have thought you still had.

This only becomes a problem if you have only, say, £200 left of your credit line (surely enough for an occasional extra on a pre-paid holiday given all the travellers' cheques you are carrying). *All* your £200 may well be blocked off, without your being made aware of this. Upon arriving at a motel cash desk you present your card, only to have the central computer in New York say that you have no credit left, not the £200 you expected. At the end of a three-week stay you may well have spent more than you expected, relying upon that £200 for the last couple of days.

Such inconvenience might even continue *after* you have returned the car intact — it takes time to unblock a blocked line of credit.

Ask exactly how much of a credit line is being blocked, and if possible, before leaving home pay off as much of the credit card debt as you can to enlarge your line of credit. And do this in enough time for the central computer to have the new state of your account before you use your card in the USA.

Rentals: any alternatives?

- **Part holiday hire.** Here you pick up your car only when you intend to travel away from your arrival area. If staying a week at Disney-world-Epcot before touring it might be worth your while to take a bus or taxi from the airport on your arrival, picking up the car only when you actually need it a week later. You'll hardly need a car at the self-sufficient Disney complex.

  Similarly if you intend to spend a final week in central New York City it might be wise to return ('check in') the hired car as soon as you arrive (after perhaps a circuit of the main highway and bridges), travelling by subway or taxi to avoid car parking costs (astronomi-cal). *But,* if you want to explore central Florida or New York's Long Island keeping the car will be essential. Don't rely upon being able to borrow friends' cars — they'll probably need them just to function normally.

- **Delivery driving.** Drive a car for someone flying long distances. Specialist companies, listed in *Yellow Pages,* will link you up with people seeking to avoid long-distance driving. Be prepared to be fingerprinted, photographed and charged a $250 deposit that will be returned when the car is produced safe and on time. The general route will be set out for you, with 300 to 400 miles per day expected. In Miami cars may well be available for New York City using I95, with small detours allowed for accommodation. For a couple with luggage this can be a godsend.

> An Aussie leaving Norfolk, Virginia, bound for Sydney by way of Los Angeles got to drive a rock-star's British registered Daimler right across country, complete with peaked cap for driver. His wife rode behind in style!

- **Motor homes.** These huge motorised caravans (also called **campers** or **RVs/recreational vehicles**) give plenty of space for a family of four, though are probably no cheaper than a car plus motel accommodation unless pre-booked as part of a bargain package. All mod-cons are standard − toilet, shower, mains-voltage generator and hook-up facilities for organised stopping sites.

  Unlike cars they usually have to be returned to the place of hire (no one-way rentals), and they only give about 10 mph. *But* they can allow you to explore of the main highways: US parks are plentiful, well kept and often have hook-up facilities, though parks such as Yosemite in California are now so popular entry has to be pre-booked very early in the year for school holiday periods.

  More importantly, staying in such parks allows you to meet ordinary middle-Americans (the famous 'Silent Majority') in fairly relaxed surroundings. Unlike the situation in impersonal motels people do mix in park camp sites, children soon find playmates, and barbecues sound to the music of the banjo and guitar. Officially alcohol is usually banned, but if no one gets silly beer (and ice!) usually appear from the huge coolers people take with them everywhere.

- **Borrowing from family or friends.** This is not usually a good idea, unless as part of a house swap. The easiest way to outstay your welcome is to have your host's car when their work, shopping and kids' routines all depend upon them having two cars. Having said that, though, Americans are amazingly generous with offering the use of their cars, albeit the second one. However it's probably only a good idea for an odd day here and there.

If you need one every day you should hire one, or re-think your visit to concentrate upon those attractions with easy car-less access, as with the museums of central Washington DC, well served by the new Metro (but even so only from certain suburbs).

TAKING THE CAR TO THE USA

In a word: DON'T. At least don't unless it is an exceptional, rare or vintage (low octane) vehicle. The shipping costs are only the start:

- If you normally use 4 star (96-8 octane) you can't buy it in the USA (US 'premium' grade is about 93 octane). Even if you have a 2 or 3 star car the use of 'premium' is expensive (by US standards).
- If you are staying more than temporarily you will have to meet very strict Federal emission regulations (or worse, California's even stricter rules). The only exceptions are for pre-1956 cars (almost vintage in US terms!) for which no modifications are required, or for pre-1966 cars for which only minor modifications to the crankcase are needed.
- Horror stories abound of cars failing to meet US standards being destroyed at the port of entry.

Words of warning:

- Even importing US-specification cars will require at least a new catalytic converter if the car has used leaded petrol in Europe.
- Though a European-bought car may get into the USA such a private import will have no US warranty, which can make repairs expensive.

As a general rule buying or hiring a car is going to be a better bet, cheaper and more convenient.

BUYING A CAR IN THE USA

This may be a very good idea if you are staying for any length of time. Japanese cars have swamped the market, are available at good prices, and spares are readily available. For Europeans Japanese cars are probably easier to handle, especially around town. The only snag may be some growing anti-Japanese feeling, though unless you are going to do business with a US car company or supplier, such feelings are unlikely to affect you. In fact as Americans become more used to Japanese cars it is quite likely that names such as Nissan will become as 'American' as Volkswagen!

British volume cars are not available in the USA, but Range Rovers,

Jaguars and Rolls-Royces are, and driving one of these will stimulate much favourable admiration. If you are using your Britishness as a selling point driving a British car may be a positive advantage. Patriotic Americans expect others to be equally patriotic.

What's good value for money?

- **Air conditioning** may seem like a luxury to those who thinks 21°C (70°F) is a heat wave. But in a hot and muggy 33°C (90°F), air conditioning can make the difference between being able to carry on or not.

Beware: Relying on moving the heat control from hot to cold will not do the job. All that happens is that hot outside air will be blown through the car without being first further heated by the engine.

There are a few snags with air conditioning:

1. It can easily put a mile per gallon onto your fuel consumption, but at US prices this is hardly worth considering (power-steering also adds a further loss).
2. In under-powered cars such as the old Ford Tempo putting on the air conditioning produced a noticeable loss of power. By summer 1986 this problem seemed to be overcome though.
3. Again, in under-powered cars the radiator may boil if the air conditioning is left on while taking the car up long mountain passes. Overloading an under-powered car to go uphill is never a good idea.

- **Size** should not be despised. Though the days of the 'gaz-guzzler' may well be over US cars are still by and large bigger than their UK equivalents. If you intend to go across country, especially with family, you will all welcome the space. If you drive a Montego in Britain do you really want to drive the equivalent of London to Leningrad in something no larger than a Metro?

  On holiday you may find that it is worthwhile to get a larger car than usual. After all, do you normally spend most of the day in the car with most of the family? A trip over to Salt Lake City from Atlanta is not a dash down the M1 to see family in Nottingham.

- **Cruise controls** are rarely available in Europe. Put simply the control is pre-set to a particular speed, say the legal 55 mph maximum. You press the button, and that's the speed you keep to up hill and down dale, come what may. To pass you can still accelerate.

Braking, or moving into a lower gear, will cancel the control, to be resumed at the touch of a button.

So why bother?

1. It does wonders for your mpg on long trips.
2. It avoids the problem familiar to long-distance drivers of gradually speeding up as the miles pass by, leading to a speeding ticket. And this does happen!
3. It makes long, smooth freeway drives less tiring, especially out west.

Buying new

Good news: As with most consumer goods cars in the USA are generally cheaper than abroad. The vastness and wealth of the market means that economies of scale can be enacted for basic features, and a wide variety of options can be available.

Bad news: The US 'sticker price' is even more misleading than in the UK. The price that caught your eye may be for the most basic model. The car actually available in the showroom already comes equipped with 'optional' extras, and these mount up. This practice is taking quite a hammering from the Japanese whose cars tend to be fully equipped as standard. *Always* check item by item that what you see is actually included in the asking price, even for foreign cars.

Buying second-hand

Many bargains can be obtained in the US as a result of the far more widespread desire to have the newest model, come what may. *But* beware:

*   Americans by and large maintain their cars far less well than comparable Europeans (ignore that well-cared-for look).
*   Used-car warranties are usually for about a month, and compared to Europe almost worthless, even when from reputable dealers.
*   The statutory protection now available in the UK is not generally available in the USA.
*   Cars in the snowbelt can suffer from killer corrosion due to the vast amounts of salt put down on the roads.
    (*Good news:* Where there is no snow, like southern California, corrosion can be negligible.)
*   Spares may be hard to come by for certain foreign cars, impossible to certain areas. Though Jaguar parts may be easy to obtain in New York City, in Manhattan, Kansas, they may be next to impossible (and so have to be sent from New York City!).
*   In certain states sales tax is payable on private sales. So if you buy a second-hand car from a colleague for $5,000 you will have to pay $250 tax (if the rate is 5%). Don't think you can conveniently

'forget' to pay this: when you go to re-register the car you'll be asked for the receipt and the 5% will be required there and then.

REPAIRS AND MAINTENANCE

Getting your car serviced can be very expensive. As elsewhere many businesses in this field are run by 'cowboys'. To avoid this trap many people resort to using the authorised dealer, though their rates may be so high as to force you back to the 'cowboys'. As a student the author tried to keep his VW Beetle on the road using the local VW dealer, but eventually had to resort to the local cut-price cowboys just to be able to pay the bills (and going overdrawn on a US account simply produces cheques that bounce).

A tune up is often the only maintenance that US cars ever get, not counting the car wash. Tune-up chains will, in theory, check the points and the timing, changing the oil and the plugs for you. But as these chains make their money by rapid turnover and the use of cheap and therefore unskilled labour, you may get better value for money learning to do these jobs yourself, or even getting the neighbour's car-mad teenager to do them for you. Otherwise it's just a case of asking friends and colleagues for their recommendations, and once you have found someone reliable, stick to them. Regular customers generally get the more reliable service.

If you are just visiting the USA car hire will take most of the strain. If the fanbelt breaks on the freeway a reputable company will come and collect you (and allow extra time at the end of the hire period to make up for lost time).

PETROL

Petrol is very cheap compared to Europe. Prices are those last seen at home over 10 years ago − almost as if OPEC had never existed. Even many economists think US prices are too low given higher world prices. For the visitor this is wonderful. Unless you drive at 90 mph over hundreds of miles daily your fuel bill will be the least of your worries. Credit cards, cash and usually dollar travellers' cheques (such as Bank America's VISA cheques) are all readily acceptable.

Most **gas stations** are now self-service. The days of the personal service are generally over, though facilities are still usually good. Most gas stations are more than that (as is becoming the case in the UK). In certain states, such as Virginia, gas stations even sell beer and wine.

Petrol is **regular** or **super,** approximately 2 or 3 star. Follow your hire car recommendations.

A word of caution: most interstate freeways do not have motorway service areas as such (though there are exceptions as along parts of the New York Thruway System) so you must leave the freeway to get petrol – hence the enormous company logos looming up in the distance as you approach an exit ramp.

- Petrol is available everywhere *but* beware of being caught short in certain areas such as national parks, especially scenic drives such as the Blue Ridge Parkway in North Carolina and Virginia. Some petrol stations do exist on such limited access tourist roads, but they are not well advertised, and you may have to leave the parkway to find petrol. Do *not* leave by the unmarked local access points or you will get hopelessly lost. Wait for the fully signposted exit (such as 'US220 to Roanoke').

- Likewise out west distances can be so vast between places large enough to have a gas station that you must be careful not to run too low, so fill up before long desert or mountain crossings. Check water and oil too. Do not leave the main road looking for services. If there were any they would be alongside the roadway, or clearly signposted. Put up your bonnet (US hood), tie a handkerchief to the aerial and wait for assistance. Sections where tourists regularly break down or run out of petrol are well known, and usually state patrol cars will turn up (eventually). Traffic going the other way may well use CB (Citizens' Band) radio to alert 'Smokey the Bear' (police) that you need assistance. Many an empty car has been found by rescue services, but with no sign of the driver, who is later found dead at some distance from the highway.

CAR INSURANCE

This is certainly essential, and mostly required these days. Rental companies will offer **collision** and **accident insurance** when you pick up the car. If staying for longer or buying your own car you really must obtain *adequate* cover. But be careful. Read *all* the small print, and ensure that you have bought the cover that you need, and that you have bought what you *think* you have bought.

The author found that his policy didn't cover the theft of the car engine on one occasion, nor on another occasion the theft of the car, presumably by 'joy-riders', and its return with several hundreds of dollars' worth of damage.

Check the arithmetic on your bill. If you have failed to pay the last dollar for whatever reason the company may well refuse to pay, and lawyers cost money to put the pressure on.

Insurance is very expensive, and it may be very tempting to obtain the minimum legal cover. Resist this temptation if at all possible. **Uninsured-driver liability insurance** may seem a luxury against a very slight and unlikely risk, but given the number of uninsured drivers it isn't. In many States where insurance is required failure to have it still only produces a derisory fine, and may only be put into effect if the driver has committed a moving violation. Premiums are usually three times higher than in the UK. Even for those with a clean driving record and 10 years behind the wheel comprehensive cover is very expensive. And if uninsured drivers are really poor you won't be able to sue them, so you do need to be insured against the uninsured.

LICENCES

Is a British driving licence valid?
Driving is a State responsibility, so the regulations change from place to place. A full British licence is valid for a year in most States, though if you take up residence you may be required to take a State test before that, say after three or six months. Usually there's a highway code test (sometimes automated, often multiple choice). Whether you then have to take a road test depends on the particular State. In the 1970s Maryland required the car to be parked neatly alongside the kerb, and little else beyond the highway code test and the fee.

Generally northern States have stricter requirements, the southern States more relaxed ones. You'll probably be asked to surrender your old British licence. If you do so you will have to tangle with the Swansea DVLC on your return. Avoid this inconvenience by saying you haven't got one to hand in.

What about the International Driving Licence?
This has a confirmation that your licence is in fact a licence, with a dozen translations, one being in Russian. As a British licence is in English it is usually okay on its own. Don't rely just upon the international one — all traffic cops and most rental clerks don't know what it is and don't intend to find out.

The only snag with a British licence is the lack of an obvious date of birth. All US licences have a date of birth (hence their use as ID to buy alcohol). Use your passport if you have to rather than explain about the expiry date being your 70th birthday (which amazes most Americans as their licences are only good for a few years usually).

If you have to move home from one State to another you'll need to reapply for a licence. Cars have to be re-registered too. If you settle down you may still have to renew both from time to time. Sometimes this is automatic, sometimes upon application (plus fee, re-test of the eyes and the highway code).

The good news is that getting a test is very easy. It may be necessary to book a test, or you may be able just to turn up on spec. Fees are nominal too. Most people pass. If you can't drive in the USA you are looked upon as eccentric as best, suspicious at worst.

Certain jurisdictions issue 'This is not a driver's permit' pieces of identification just so that people who don't drive for whatever reason can carry ID with their full date of birth and full name in a government issued format.

WORDS OF WARNING

Driving in the USA can be a relaxing activity in a large, air-conditioned car along the interstate highway out in the countryside. But in cities, especially at rush hour, it can be a nightmare. The width of roads and parking spaces, the use of power steering, and the cheapness of the petrol can all make driving part of the holiday *but* in heavy traffic many US drivers are far from competent.

Cars crowd together even more than in Britain, driving far too close to the car ahead in rush hour traffic. Overtaking takes place on all sides, which can be very alarming even to drivers used to heavy London traffic or the M6 through the West Midlands (Europe's heaviest traffic at rush hour). Drivers of large trucks often drive right up behind cars and intimidate them right out of the way.

After two weeks leisurely driving across the South arriving in the Washington DC area can be a nightmare at almost any time of day: the traffic is likely to seem aggressive, fast, and far too close together. The use of the metro (the underground railway) suddenly becomes very appealing.

And *always* drive defensively.

TRAFFIC REGULATIONS

Generally these are the same as those you are familiar with at home, though with some tricky variations to keep you on your toes. **Round-abouts** hardly exist, except in a few larger cities, and then only at the junction of large boulevards. If they are called anything it will be **rotaries.** Of course they are anticlockwise, often confusing to those of us who normally drive on the left and are used to giving directions clockwise.

Traffic lights are usually called **stop lights.** Their location can take some getting used to as they are generally on the far side of the intersection to which they refer. Draw up to them at your peril: you will soon find that your rear end is stuck blocking the intersection behind you. There are also a number of interesting complications.

- **Flashing red or orange** – beware! This means a four-way stop (see below) but with someone having the right of way. At night a main city avenue may well have flashing amber at every intersection. Go through with the right of way, but beware of crossing traffic. Flashing red means that someone else has the flashing orange right of way. Stop. Cross or turn only when safe to do so. Fortunately this system only operates when traffic is sparse, such as in the early hours of the morning.

- **No turn on red** means that when there is a red light traffic may not turn right. Though this may seem blindingly self-evident to a newly arrived visitor, it actually tells drivers that the normal rule is for traffic to turn right when there is a red light so long as they have come to a full halt and it is clear to do do. Most, but not all the states, have this rule. Beware of cities that have spread over state lines. Different rules may apply on either side of the state line.

- **Right lane must turn** is a delightful invitation to turn at right angles to the direction you have been going, and it is compulsory. If you have stayed in such a lane too long and try to go straight on you will find you get a ticket, at best, or a punch-up with irate drivers you block in when you find that by going straight ahead you've come up against no available lane. Even when the lane you want is blocked by roadworks you must obey the signs for your particular lane, or risk the consequences. The author was physically assaulted in just such a case.

- **Four-way stops** require *all* traffic to stop, but the driver there first *from whatever direction* has the right of way. In case of a dead heat give way to traffic coming from the right. Numerous local variations exist, which can be quite a trial for the outsider. For a **two-way stop** one road has the right of way, and on a **three-way stop** only one direction has the right of way, all others must come to a halt. The signs all look superficially much the same, and may not be placed in the most obvious position. Usually, though, these arrangements are only found in residential neighbourhoods away from the main roads.

As with so many directions in the USA literacy is assumed. Only reluctantly have pictograms (such as are used in international signs) been introduced, even in tourist or immigrant areas.

Since the New Deal of the late 1930s paved roads have been built even in the most out of the way areas. Nevertheless vast areas of the West still have gravel or even dirt roads. Through-travellers will probably see little of this though. Motorways are generally well maintained, and at a far better standard than found in many cities.

The winter snows sweep much further south (occasionally even to the Gulf of Mexico) than you might expect. Traffic in the northern States usually adjusts fairly smoothly, but where snow is a novelty traffic can be crazy, with people driving both too fast or far too slowly. Snow-tyres are required in many States, both to avoid a ticket from the highway patrol, and simply to get about. Snow-chains may be essential in out of the way areas and in ski-resorts.

Speeding

Officially speed limits are set by each State, not the Federal government. However, the Federal government can withold Federal highway grants from States not agreeing to enforce Federal standards on inter-state highways (almost all of the motorway standard dual-carriageway). The 55 mph speed limit has thus become a national limit, but one rarely observed within metropolitan areas or in the vast distances out west. Buried traffic monitors record the proportion of traffic obeying the 55 mph limit, and States lose highway grants if more than half of passing traffic is over the limit. Paying State patrolmen to slow the traffic down can become fiscally necessary given the expense of highway maintenance. So a guerrilla war rumbles on between CB radio-equipped truckers and state patrol cars ('Smokey the Bear'). Western States periodically attempt to have the limits changed, or threaten to ignore the limit and take the consequences.

In towns limits are usually 35-40 mph, but watch for local variations, often set to catch the unwary outsider who can then be required to pay a fine or post bail on the spot (which amounts to much the same). Obey all limits, at least until you have been in an area long enough to get a feel for how the traffic locally responds to them. At corners there are often advisory limits (on a yellow background). In the mountains limits tend to be both realistically set and observed (drivers who don't observe them don't survive).

Parking

Parking downtown can be as bad as in central London. Fortunately, though, many downtown banks and stores have their own free or subsidised parking lots. Parking meters are often available, and feeding the meter is permitted if you dash out in time. Regular parking, though, can be very expensive, and is often only available for all-day commuters with season tickets. You can see cars being parked by attendants in the reverse order their owners can be expected to come and collect them at the end of the day.

Certain areas have surprisingly large parking areas available. Washington DC's central Mall, around which many sights and most of the museums cluster, has parking areas just for visitors, though in high season these will fill early on, and using the metro may well be a better idea.

ALTERNATIVES TO DRIVING

Do visitors have to drive everywhere? Fortunately not, for alternatives do exist:

- buses, both long distance and local
- underground systems
- taxis
- walking
- flying
- trains.

The most exotic of these is undoubtedly walking. *Time* (the US news magazine) had an article in September 1987 on how the British *of all ages* still actually do it for fun! Is there no end to British eccentricity?

Long distance buses

The most well-known networks are **Trailways** and **Greyhound**, soon perhaps to be amalgamated. They seem comparable in almost every way, though as yet their tickets are not interchangeable. Their networks are similar, though there may well be local variations. Unfortunately the number of towns served has declined substantially over the last few years as cross-route subsidies have been phased out, leaving the major cities well served, but unfashionable areas now served by neither train nor bus.

Though the 99 days for $99 are long since gone fares are generally quite low, though the vast distances may disguise this. Bus stations are usually in the older parts of the town, so long bus trips can be a salutary reminder of the underside of US life. Rest stops may be at peculiar times of the day or night, often in out of the way fast food strips in the middle of nowhere, a plot to make the British traveller suddenly start to appreciate motorway cafes back home!

Advantages:

- see a slice of the USA you might not otherwise come across, which includes a motley collection of passengers. Remember the opening and closing scenes in *Midnight Cowboy*?
- comparatively cheap, especially if you bought the ticket overseas
- efficient, clean and tidy, with on-board WC
- good luggage facilities (far more than by plane, which may make the trip worthwhile by itself).

Disadvantages:

- slow (comparatively)
- can be very boring for cross-country travel
- bus stations have seen better days (and may be intimidating for women and children).

Contact:

- Greyhound: (01)839 5591

Underground railways (subways)
These exist in only a minority of US cities, and those that do exist vary enormously:

- *Bay Area Rapid Transit System (BART)* is clean, reasonably priced, and an efficient way to cross the San Francisco Bay to cities such as Oakland and to certain suburbs, though many places are only linked in with feeder bus services.

- *Washington Metro* serves Washington DC with the surrounding suburban communities in northern Virginia and Maryland. Despite the rapid expansion of the suburban economy over the last 20 years this brand new system focuses upon the governmental city centre, and its radial routes serve only certain select communities, so cross-town travel remains difficult and certain parts of the city, and of the metropolis at large, remain inaccessible. Beware of the network maps which show the system as it may one day be, not as it is now. But for all that it is cheap, very efficient, crime, garbage and smoke free, and certainly on a par with Europe's better systems. Only the new Kiev system is supposedly better.

- *New York City's subway* system is cheap, vast, quite scary at times, very dirty, and an amazingly efficient way of travelling around to avoid the congested streets above. Four million people use it every day. The 230 miles of track are the amalgamation of once separate systems, which can lead to quite complex interchange stations. For travelling around Manhattan it is excellent as the buses get bogged down in the traffic. For Long Island the service is not so good, though there is an express route using modern trains to and from the nearest station to John F Kennedy airport.

Some systems are not underground at all, but as in Boston and Chicago elevated (as was the case in much of the New York network originally). The 'El' helped blight large areas around the downtown. To get some idea of what it must have been like having to live near such overhead systems watch the John Belushi and Don Akroyd 1980 movie *Blues Brothers* set in modern Chicago.

At some suburban stations you may see 'Kiss and Ride' signs, pull-in bays for drivers to let off commuting spouses. Park and ride facilities are also available at certain suburban stations.

Taxis

These are more likely to be of use in the more European cities of the east then in the more American cities of the west. In New York City it may be actually quicker to walk 10 or even 15 blocks given the traffic, though a cab ride will ensure that you don't arrive wet through. Summers are long and very sticky. Winters are often very snowy. Taxis are metered, but don't expect cab drivers to be able to change large denomination notes. Many drivers may not speak English, and may have little if any knowledge of anywhere outside the major destinations. In certain cities only certain cabs are allowed to drive over the city boundary, so check before the meter starts. In the national capital a drive to most suburban communities involves crossing over into the next state, foreign territory to many inner city drivers.

Remember: Many cities are as large as London, and taxi rides across Los Angeles or New York City can be very expensive indeed. You can arrange to take a vehicle that is half way between a cab and and a bus – a **limousine.** These long huge cars may take half a dozen travellers plus baggage from out-of-town communities to the airport for bus-like fares for a taxi-like service. Check *Yellow Pages*, and book in advance.

Long distance taxi rides are possible, but very expensive. It would usually be cheaper to hire a car and drive yourself. But in a domestic airline strike, for instance, such long distance rides to another international airport that is open may turn out to be essential. Get a price *before* the trip starts, though.

Walking

This is an art, one that has all but been given up except for a hardy few.
Attempting to walk off a Christmas dinner a group of Britons living for a
while in northern Virginia were picked up by the local police, though
perhaps more out of curiosity than any attempt at harassment. Suburban neighbourhoods may well lack sidewalks altogether. Paths lead only
from the house to the kerb! Certain neighbourhoods may be suspicious
of any strangers, especially those on foot.

Some downtowns now encourage shoppers to use the shoppers' bus
between the main shopping intersections. This encourages less walking
per person, but probably helps raise the actual number of people walking along the streets. In hot and humid cities learn to walk down that
side of the street giving some shade. Whatever the season work on the
general assumption that car drivers cannot see you. Never assume a
right of way, even at marked crossing areas (British style zebra or
pelican crossings don't exist). But walking across as and where you will
may result in a ticket for jay-walking (even in the deserted downtown on
a Sunday morning if your luck has run out).

Overall walking is okay for young people, especially when combined
with buses and subway trains. But it is not feasible for most families, if
only for the extremes of heat and cold. Downtowns can be less than
safe, and distances great. The central mall of Washington DC is decepti-
vely laid out. Distances from monument to monument can be enormous, and with children impossible. The DC police patrols have been
known to use bull horns to warn twilight pedestrians to leave the open
spaces immediately for their own safety! And darkness comes much
more swiftly than in northern countries such as Britain.

Flying

Flying is cheap per mile by European standards, but as distances are
vast prices can still seem very expensive. Standby tickets are available,
though around public holidays all seats will have been long since booked
up. But given the sheer size of the USA flying is often the only way to
travel any distance within the time available.

Traditionally the USA has had a network of international, regional
and local companies, nested together to provide a service to most places
within the USA. The cost of this overly cosy arrangement was seen as a
lack of competition, higher than necessary prices, and an over-extended
network necessarily subsidised by higher than desirable fares on the
most popular routes.

Deregulation of routes has caused a major change in air travel.
Popular routes attracted new services at lower fares, so forcing large
companies to follow. Conversely many smaller places have lost their

services altogether. Even large companies have gone bankrupt, been taken over, or have merged. The situation is still, and may well remain, in flux.

The implication for visitors is that whereas it has become cheaper and generally more convenient to fly into and out of large metropolitan areas (where, after all, most people live) it may be difficult to fly on to specific, smaller destinations. Relatives who could once have met you at Cullowhee airport North Carolina (a small college town in the Great Smoky Mountains) may how have to go to Ashville some 40 miles away across the mountains, though as a freeway has just opened on this route this is now no real hardship. They may even prefer to drive some hundreds of miles south to Atlanta for the novelty of meeting you at the international airport. Few Americans get any opportunity to meet arriving foreigners, so may be eager to travel to meet you.

Book from the UK whenever possible to take advantage of special rates not available within the USA, especially for your transatlantic carrier (or affiliated airlines in the USA). Various packages are periodically on offer, with a series of vouchers being purchased that can be exchanged for tickets, or a fare-arranged schedule that is guaranteed but inflexible. In the winter months transatlantic carriers often offer special internal rates to attract custom. These are advertised in the Sunday papers, particularly if business has dipped for some reason (as in 1986 with exchange rate changes and fear of terrorism in Europe).

Fly-drive
With an 'open-jaw' ticket this enables you to fly into one city, drive to another, and fly home without having to drive all the way back: great for cross-country trips. Two weeks across country from New York City to Los Angeles, with a week in each place as well can be an ideal introduction to the USA. The extra drop-off charge at least means you don't have to dash back to New York City, and can instead spend a leisurely week in California before flying home.

The price might be:

Half the return APEX to New York City	+
Half the return APEX from Los Angeles	+
Two weeks car hire (carrier's special offer)	+
Drop-off charge	+
Insurance premiums	+

Accommodation in each city and *en route*.

Air-travel seasons
These are rooted as much in the calendar as in the weather. For travel purposes three unfamiliar seasons appear:

- Low – off peak, especially term time
- High – summer holidays
- Shoulder – late November (Thanksgiving)

Summer is set by convention having almost the power of law. It opens
with Memorial Day in late May and lasts until Labor Day in early
September. To get, for instance, student rates after Labor Day may
necessitate having convincing ID (identification papers) as all US students will then be back in school (or college).

Trains
Trains do travel the length and breadth of the USA, but services are less
frequent and serve fewer places since motorways and flying have taken
most of the long distance passengers. Despite the poor state of repair of
much of the remaining network using the train has certain major advantages over flying or driving:

- seeing the country from an increasingly unfamiliar perspective that
  cannot possibly be provided by high altitude flying;
- it is relaxing not having to do the driving;
- it is useful for travellers going from one downtown to another, such
  as tourists or certain business people.

Unfortunately only a railway enthusiast would want to do the whole
cross-country journey, if only because of the timetable implications, not
to mention the length of time involved.

It is still worthwhile taking one of the more popular sections of the
network, which is now run by Amtrak. This semi-nationalised passenger network tries to keep the passenger services going, but is restricted
to using other people's track, which is maintained to a variety of standards. Trains may have to crawl through certain areas to avoid track
collapse, only to speed effortlessly away once back onto a commercially
maintained freight network. Compared to the European system the
Amtrak network is very rudimentary. Only in the northeast's Boston to
Washington DC corridor does it have anything like an Inter-City feel
about it.

Useful links connect the New York City based corridor north to
Canada (which has its own full system quite unlike the US) and south to
Florida. With careful planning it is still possible to go over to Chicago or
down to New Orleans. Changing trains and spending four days *en route*
can enable the hardy traveller to reach the West Coast at a leisurely 40
mph. Once in Los Angeles there is a well-used service south to San
Diego.

For travellers on the Atlantic seaboard bound for the Pacific Northwest it is probably better to go north to Montreal in Canada, take the

trans-Canada system west to Vancouver, and then go south again into the USA. The service is good (though not so elegant as it once was) and the scenery is spectacular.

Amtrak's **Southwest Chief** runs from Chicago to Los Angeles (and back again). Speeds rarely reach 70 mph, but this enables riders to relax as the scenery rolls gently by. This route is something of a flagship for Amtrak's long-distance routes, with quite a high level of service, which includes films, leaflets on points of interest, and even speakers to talk about the areas being crossed. On-board facilities are appropriate for people used to travelling long distance by Greyhound, if not quite up to airline standards. Coaches are on two levels. The lower level has several airline-type toilets, changing rooms, luggage storage, and seating areas for those who find it difficult to negotiate the stairs to the upper deck. There is also a formal dining-car and a cafeteria, though as with captive markets everywhere prices are not cheap, with full meals starting at about $12 a head. A steak dinner would cost about $25 a head with wine. One of the advantages of this particular journey is that a stopover at Flagstaff, Arizona, can be made. Take a hired car (or even hitch as I did) north to the nearby Grand Canyon, truly one of the wonders of the world.

Unfortunately this level of service is not yet provided on all other long-distance services. For the 30 plus hours from Los Angeles to Seattle only a basic service is provided, there are generally more people, but watching the landscape change and talking to fellow passengers is usually enough to while away the hours. Some places that you might expect to be on the system aren't, such as San Francisco, but the trains do call at Oakland across the Bay, with connecting buses available.

If you would like to get the feel of what it is like to arrive in a small western town by train, to step down onto the side of the tracks only to watch the train leave you standing in the middle of nowhere read Malcolm Bradbury's novel *Stepping Westward* published in 1965, now an Arena paperback at £2.25.

Practical train information.
A complicated (British Rail style) discount structure means groups get a better rate than any individual, but for the rugged individualist there are some packages:

- **14 day regional tickets** for the Northeast $125 (1986 prices)

East	$215
Far West	$125
West	$225

- **30 day pass** to include Florida $ 45

- **USA Rail Pass** 14 days $375
                  21 days $450
                  30 days $525

To give you some idea of ordinary prices:

- New York City to Montreal $ 35
- New York City to Miami $ 80
- Seattle to San Francisco $ 70
- Los Angeles to Las Vegas $ 29

For more detailed information contact:

- **Albany Travel,** 190 Deansgate, MANCHESTER M3 3ND ((061) 833 0202)
- **American Express Holidays,** Portland House, Stag Place, Victoria Street, LONDON SW1E 5BH ((01) 834 5555)

TIME ZONES

North America stretches over eight and a half time zones. When it's noon in Alaska it's 7.30 pm in Newfoundland. As you travel west you 'gain' time. If you drive from Pittsburgh to Denver you may well leave at 10 am one day and arrive at 10 am the next, driving straight through. But the journey will have taken 26 hours. If you go from west to east you 'lose', so if you left Denver at 10 am and arrived at Pittsburgh the following day at 10 am it would have taken you 22 hours (maybe you missed the traffic driving in this direction and saved a few hours!)

Most Americans, however, live within a four zone world, from Atlantic to Pacific. Eastern Standard Time is five hours behind Greenwich, Central six hours, Mountain seven, and Pacific eight. So midday in London is 7 am in New York City, 6 am in Chicago, 5 am in Denver, and 4 am in Los Angeles. This is complicated by two factors:

- **Daylight Saving Time** which operates much the same as Summer Time in the UK. However, certain States refuse to use it, so watch out in Arizona, Hawaii and parts of Indiana.
- The switch-over is on the last Sunday in April, which is not usually the date(s) used in Europe.

Actually there is a third complication: the refusal to use the 24-hour clock (except perhaps in the military). Timetables will only use the 12-hour clock, with bold type for times after noon. This has confused many overseas arrivals who think there are no trains, planes, buses in the afternoon on the very route they want to make! It makes you realise how even the 24-hour clock, like metric temperature, gradually catches up with even the most dyed in the wool Brit.

TRAVELLING WITH THE KIDS

The USA is a wonderful place for families. From the moment you arrive you'll realise that it's still a more child-oriented society:

- most hire cars have rear seat-belts fitted as standard, and major agencies can provide safety seats for young children
- most motels let children share their parents' room without extra charge (and most rooms have two double-beds anyway as standard)
- restaurants keep high-chairs or booster-seats ready, and children's menus are common. Colouring books may emerge from folded children's menus too!

Don't despair! Children's food is not compulsory for adults. All-you-can eat meals (a speciality in certain chains) have everything from sugar-puffs to spicy sausages at breakfast, via scrambled eggs, muffins and juices. Breakfasts are good value and usually provide something for everyone to feast upon.

Theme parks, whether Disneyworld and Seaworld in central Florida, or Dollywood in east Tennessee's Smoky Mountains, are for children of all ages; young children aren't ignored; and parents needn't feel like social outcasts for turning up with their offsprings. Even more 'serious' places such as the science museums of Washington DC encourage children to touch, watch puppet shows, and generally behave like children. National Parks, such as the Rocky Mountain and Mesa Verde Parks in Colorado, have talks and activities especially for children.

Snags
It would be foolish to suggest travelling with children turns up no problems:

- Summer heat can be so overwhelming that the car may become the only haven of air-conditioning (and thus sanity) for all the family. But distances on cross-country trips can be extremely demoralising. A sufficiently large car is essential for all concerned.
- Motels rarely have anywhere for children to play, nor are playmates available as would be possible staying with friends or in a country hotel.

Good news
Overall most visitors would say the good outweighs the bad:

- At least there's television (morning cartoons are everywhere, not just for a few minutes as in the UK). Most motels have a pool (check *before* booking to avoid disappointment). After being cooped up for long periods in the car a pool is usually very welcome by everyone.

- Standards of hygiene are high throughout the USA; bathrooms with showers are standard in all motel rooms; disposable nappies (diapers) are at every drugstore; and the locals by and large speak English (for when the fan-belt breaks late at night as you are crossing the South).

- Toys are excellent. Well, the range and price of toys is very good. In fact the range (and volume) of toys is as likely to startle you as the viciousness of the war toys. If you haven't seen a large toy shop in the UK for 30 years you'd probably get a shock! Use the local Yellow Pages to find the nearby 'Toys R Us', part of a vast chain of toys-only supermarkets giving both good value and great variety.

- Children do enjoy the USA. Even young children will both cope with and enjoy it (though maybe more or less than anywhere in Europe). Swimming together at the end of each day's travelling or exertions remains a fond memory for years after. Even surviving the ferocious summer heat becomes a well-earned battle scar. Also, for adults taking children can provide an open sesame to people and places you'd never otherwise visit.

Even if you do intend to take your family for an extended stay and wish first to try out living together in the USA it might be worth considering house-swapping rather than a touring holiday.

Tick those items you'd think would provide good experience of what it would be like to live (rather than holiday) in the USA:

touring holiday	**house-swapping**
on the move	stay in one place
motels	house with garden
eating out	eating both out and in
always together	more flexibility
strangers	neighbours
always something new	return to base each day

Books of advice

As there are more and more parents taking more and more children abroad there are ever more how-to-do-it guides. Those worth looking at include:

- David Haslam, *Travelling with Children: A Survival Guide for Parents,* published by Macdonald, London, 1987, has readable and authoritative sections on planning, safe car and air travel, strategies for journeys, eating and drinking, burns, bites and bugs. It's a useful introduction for anyone considering going abroad with children, for however long.

- A similar paperback is Pamela Hyde's *Holidays with Kids,* Piatkus, London, 1987, which is very general, but has useful and reassuring sections on keeping children entertained, fed and healthy, besides sections on choosing which type of holiday is appropriate for particular families, a vital consideration for such long-haul visits as to the USA. There is little specifically geared to US travel as such, but its general approach is useful.

- *Have Kids, Will Travel* is an excellent guide by Susan Grossman, published by Christopher Helm, London 1987. It is excellent value for money, well written and presented, with some useful thoughts about types of US holidays for children. As with the other books mentioned in this section it is a general introduction and guide, but none the less useful for that. Since such general advice doesn't age quickly you may find that you can use copies in the local public library.

8
Finding Work

There are two major reasons for going to any foreign country:

- interest
- job or career

Of course you can make a holiday of a student summer camp job, and you may have taken up a job just to follow up your interest in the USA. But though all reasons are in some ways interconnected it helps to establish what your priorities are if you sort out in your own mind what the main reason is. If it is a relaxing holiday then don't undermine that perfectly reasonable aim by being on the telephone all the time trying to set up useful business links!

Short-term options for young people will be dealt with later in Chapter 11. Let's look now at the various possibilities for those who don't have to be back for next term or for a purely UK job.

STAYING IN THE USA FOR FUN

Many people find going abroad is something for the young, with few ties, between college and going to work. But consider the alternatives:

Staying in Britain	Going to the USA
Getting into a career	Getting experience of life.
Getting into the housing market	Not being tied down by a mortgage
Having a family while fit and young	Being more flexible and able to take risks
Getting a job while they are still available	Expanding your horizons
Building up seniority in a firm	Gaining useful confidence
Becoming a sober, hard-working citizen	Changing job tracks

Now add your own counter arguments in the spaces provided! Once you've done that, choose which options are for you. If most are in the **left-hand** column:

- you could work hard at home but holiday in the USA
- you could try for some US-based experience with your firm
- you could house-swap for three to four weeks one year.

If most are in the **right-hand** column:

- consider taking a degree in the USA
- take a long trip with casual work
- consider what foreign experience would interest an employer when you got back.

Career advantages of a stint in the USA

The universities, polytechnics and colleges pour out new graduates each and every year, each waving their newly minted degrees. Three hundred applications for a single job is not an unusual situation. How can you stand out from the crowd?

Everyone wants someone with experience, but if no one will give you that initial chance it can all seem futile. But take heart: a new employer's interests may be raised by an applicant who has travelled, not aimlessly, but in relation to their field of interest. Political science students who've spent a term at a college in Washington DC have something no amount of pulling pints in the students' union bar over the vacation can provide.

A three month stint working in the USA offers an employer someone with just a suggestion of adaptability, initiative and a willingness to try something different, unafraid of trying something new. A stint in the USA may be the only thing separating you from the pack when a short-list is drawn up. And being a year or so older than the rest of the pack when you return may also be in your favour — you are just that bit more mature, that bit more self-reliant, and so should need just that bit less supervision. And employers like that.

Of course you may be looking to the USA for a more long-term job rather than a stint overseas to help you once back in Britain. Many British people do exceptionally well in the USA, from butlers to athletes, but don't expect the USA to provide increased career prospects, a better material standard of living, or just a good time by virtue of your arrival with a British accent. If you don't like hard work, long hours, and a lot of knocks, the USA isn't going to do much for you except see your time and money slip away.

Working for fun

If you want to be able to return to the USA you need to be legal. See Chapter 5 on visas for how this can be done. But the best laid schemes come adrift and you may find yourself out of money far from friends or the airport. Summer harvesting, working in bars, helping friends move or decorate, acting as a nanny: all can pay well, but the longer you remain within the black economy the more risky it'll become. If you do it only for a few weeks before moving on little risk will exist, but it's still illegal, and though it's possible to get the ever necessary ID (identification) via driving licences (US 'driver's license'), social security number and bank accounts it's an increasingly risky business.

The degree of paranoia this lifestyle can produce can be gauged by a recent non-event in New York City. The Immigration and Naturalization Service (INS) estimated that there are some 70,000 illegal Irish residents within this one city alone. An amnesty was declared: 'Make yourself known and you'll be allowed to "regularize" your status'. Two (yes, that's 2) people turned up at the INS. The source of this story has been checked with RTE (Irish Radio, 7 May 1987, Gay Byrne morning show).

Beware: if you think that the worst that can happen is for the INS to catch you and deport you remember:

- the Internal Revenue Service (IRS) will first want their back tax before they'll let you leave the USA
- if you want to return to the USA you need a statement on your exit papers that you are not a tax delinquent, even if the IRS and INS will let you go this time.

Remember: It was not the FBI that got Al Capone. It was the IRS who put him away for non-payment of taxes!

THE BUSINESS CULTURE IN THE USA

'It is a sad fact of life that many people who go to work abroad, either on secondment to an overseas branch or subsidiary of a UK employer or on contract to a truly overseas company, give less thought to their circumstances than they would if they were simply to be going abroad on holiday for a few weeks.'

Harry Brown in *Working Abroad?*, 1986

Join another company, go to another school, or just change jobs and we're likely to find that many more things have changed besides our physical surroundings. Even if our job description remains much the same the way things work around us may change, sometimes so subtly that at first we don't notice what's going on. But soon we find people interpret rules slightly differently, a pleasant surprise when it's in our favour, but a bit of a shock when we seem to lose out. Expectations may be a bit different. How we bend the rules changes. In fact it's a little bit like being in another country. Those who study businesses say that each business has its own culture. How much more potentially confusing when the change of job is compounded with a change of country! Two cultures, one large, one small, change both at once, and we're expected to adjust without missing a step.

So it's easy to see why staying with the same company if you are moving countries can be a great advantage, particularly if the style of management remains the same. If you have been 'Americanised' during your time already with the company then moving to the USA will not be such a jump into the complete unknown.

If American companies pay well they do so because they expect quite a lot. This is a capitalist dog-eat-dog economy, which though not averse to protectionist barriers and government handouts still has a more raw edge to its business dealings than in Britain.

> *A word of warning:* Don't be taken in by those firms that have a laid-back, casual air about them. These mainly new firms, especially in software and the media, can be just as efficient and hardnosed when they want to be, and if your presence turns out to be a waste of space they'll 'let you go' (fire you!).

Being British means having certain immediate assumptions made about you. Your accent (whether Geordie, Liverpuddlian or Sloane, it matters not) will be seen as very formal, which will confirm their expectation of you as dour, a bit stand-offish, especially out west (where the author has been taken for a Boston, Massachusetts, native, the distinction between England and New England being a little too subtle for certain laid-back West Coast residents!). Unless you really are pompous, colleagues are quite likely to tell you, say in the bar round the corner during Friday's happy hour, that you're not as stuffily formal as they'd expected. This will be a personal point, and will in no way change their beliefs that everyone else back in Britain is a stuffed shirt.

The greatest shock for most Britons starting work in the USA is due to the long hours and short holidays. The business culture demands it (and thinks it essential to continued prosperity even though the West Germans tend to have five or six weeks holidays and are at least as prosperous!).

Long hours

The *minimum* working week in the USA is often still 40 hours (not the 38 so popular in the UK), the 8 hours per day meaning just that, with people expected to be at their seats working away bang on 9 am, and not leaving until precisely 5 pm. There's no five minutes grace, and certainly no couple of hours off for the dentist, unless sick-leave is first agreed.

This may be how your UK office was run, so it wouldn't be quite the surprise it is to some. What may be a surprise is that many people start earlier, at 8 am. Colleges usually schedule their first classes at 8 am, and having to discuss the finer points of a course so early can be quite a shock to the British visitor. Colleges too may schedule classes to start as late as 7 pm, so for some academics it can be a long day.

Holidays

The real surprise comes over holidays. In the first year employees may receive no holidays except for the 6 public holidays required by law, a week if they are lucky, two weeks if very lucky indeed. Each year of employment raises the entitlement by a day, but it may take some years to gain a three week break. Academics expecting an Easter vacation will find there isn't one, and the long summer vacation is often unpaid, so it's necessary and expected that you'll teach summer school, intensive courses for people either in a hurry to graduate, trying to catch up or having to repeat a failed course.

Bad news time

US public holidays are *not* necessarily 'long weekends'. Only Memorial Day (the last Monday in May) and Labor Day (the first Monday in September) are always part of a weekend, and as the first and last days of the summer season these weekends are good days to avoid freeways, airports and resorts. Christmas Day, New Year's Day, and Independence Day (July 4th) obviously can fall on any day of the week, and the days to the nearest weekend are *not* necessarily holidays (Boxing Day is unheard of so expect to work the day after Christmas Day!). Service and retail employees will probably have to work most holidays (except Christmas and New Year's Day), albeit on overtime rates.

Sick leave

This is usually only gained after a probationary period with the firm, say three months. You'll be lucky to get 5 days a year for long service. When changing companies negotiate to keep your sick leave entitlement if at all possible. Remember too that sick leave involves any time off for medical reasons, not just being on your death bed.

The contract

The USA is a country where litigation is endemic. If things don't turn out how you expected it will be very difficult to play the litigation game to your advantage without the protection of a carefully prepared contract. If you came expecting full medical cover for yourself and for your family, plus a company car, first make certain it's all in the contract, and legally watertight. Fine words butter no parsnips, or as Sam Goldwyn (of MGM fame) warned: 'A verbal contract ain't worth the paper its written on.'

Compassionate leave

Try to keep the length of your stay under your own control. If your family, particularly ageing relatives, are still in the UK you need to be able to leave your job and the USA for pressing reasons. If you are under contract with an over-the-odds salary you may not be allowed compassionate leave short of quitting and taking the consequences. Longstanding employees are more likely to be able to obtain emergency leave. Read your contract carefully. If a US company pays you over the odds (salary plus a moving allowance) they aren't going to be too happy about your leaving for any reason, especially for an open-ended period.

WORK PROSPECTS IN THE US ECONOMY

Whether going to the United States for temporary or long-term work it is useful, if not essential, to know something about the US economy, particularly which skills the job market requires, and equally as vital, *where* these jobs can be found. The US economy is so large and the country so vast that without even the most rudimentary awareness of what is going on you will be like someone blindfold in a china shop.

The traditional view of the US economy saw a great industrial heartland from Boston south to Baltimore and west over the Appalachians to Chicago. Here lived most Americans once the US had been settled from coast to coast. After the Second World War the west coast, particularly California, became a major rival to the northeast, given its entertainment industries, defence industries and increasingly its aerospace industries. The south was seen as poor, rural and hostile to black people, Roman Catholics, and in fact most outsiders. The industrial midwest merged into the prairie and thinly settled mountains. Alaska far to the northwest remained a barren, frozen waste, and Hawaii a tropical paradise somewhere in mid-Pacific.

Gradually this picture has changed as the global role of oil changed. As OPEC pushed up oil prices domestic suppliers in Texas, Oklahoma and Louisiana became very wealthy, able to invest in the further industrialisation of what came to be called the Sunbelt. Prosperity moved west to link up with southern California, and eastwards into Florida where tourism, aerospace and retirement developments forged a major rival to the once dominant northeast.

The oil crisis that boosted the Sunbelt exposed the old decaying industrial bases of what came to be known as the Rustbelt, or Snowbelt: cars, shipbuilding, machine tools all collapsed as foreign competition took vast slices of the US market. Unemployment rose to levels unknown since the dark days of the Great Depression of the 1930s. This view of a prosperous southern rim and a decaying northeast is still widely held. But beware: just as it takes its place in the public's 'mental map' of the US economy the map changes.

The 1980s have seen the farmers of the Mississippi valley plagued with over-production and falling prices. Like the heavy industrial cities of Appalachia and the Great Lakes before them they have hit bankruptcy, dispossession and decay. In contrast California still retains its prosperity, at least from Silicon Valley just south of San Francisco to Orange County in southern Los Angeles. The oil price decline of the mid 1980s has undermined the once assured prosperity of Alaska, Oklahoma, Texas and Louisiana. Unemployment here has risen dramatically above average levels, and is especially high for those in exploration and drilling concerns.

The US government policies that produced the economic boom of the early 1980s left a huge $200 billion national debt, slowing growth nationally to a barely perceptible crawl. But in California and along the Atlantic coast growth persists at four per cent per year from 1981 to 1985. The midwest, whether rural or once industrial, has for the first time replaced the south as the region with the lowest incomes. Agriculture, oil and declining heavy industry ('smokestack' industries in US journalism) have all lost ground, pulling the great Mississippi-Great Lakes heartland down. High-technology and service industries such as banking, insurance and advertising have enabled the coastal states to pull ahead.

The importance of this for would-be job seekers can be gauged in the growing migration of many Americans away from places such as Texas. Don't expect jobs to be available for the asking in Dallas, whatever the TV series would still suggest. Don't even assume that investment in these areas will automatically hit pay dirt. Retrenchment of people's incomes puts often fatal pressure on small entrepreneurs.

It is these recurrent fluctuations in demands for certain skills that explains the US Immigration Service's rules requiring emigrants to have a specific job prior to the granting of immigrant status. A skill by itself might well not be sufficient, and might threaten the jobs of existing workers in a dwindling job market.

Finding out about the US economy

Here are some magazines and newspapers (often available in public and university or polytechnic libraries) that regularly carry articles on the US economy. How many of them do you read?

		regularly	*occasionally*	*never*
The 'quality' press	*The Guardian* *The Times* *The Daily Telegraph* *The Independent*			
US papers available in Europe	*The Herald Tribune* *Christian Science Monitor* *USA Today*			
US-based news magazines available in Europe	*Time Magazine* *Newsweek* *US News & World Report*			

Look at the pattern of your answers. Do you think it would be useful to read the business section of more newspapers and news magazines?

What other sources are there for more detailed information on specific sectors of the US economy or even for individual corporations? You should be prepared to investigate:

- trade magazines
- magazines of professional associations
- specific interest magazines.

To do this you need to explore not just the racks of magazines at the biggest W H Smiths or Menzies that you can find, but also to seek out your local big city public library, the reference room of your local polytechnic, and the periodicals section of your nearest university library. The range of professional and trade journals is almost limitless. You will be amazed to see computer journals from Australia, ceramic association newsletters from the USA, even Soviet journals in translations.

For a standard textbook view try Sam Rosenberg's *American Economic Development Since 1945,* Macmillan, Basingstoke, 1985. And for an excellent, speculative and highly personal look at the prospects for the post-industrial economic order see Robert B Reich, *The Next Ame-*

rican Frontier: A Provocative Program for Economic Renewal, Penguin, Harmondsworth, 1984.

WORK: PRELIMINARY CONSIDERATIONS

The whole complex issue of US entry visas has been dealt with in Chapter 5, but jobs and visas do need to be considered together. So here are a few facts to be going along with.

Who can take a US job?
Only those allowed to live in the USA for compassionate reasons, whether to reunite families or to obtain asylum, are generally speaking allowed to take whatever job they can.

Everyone else must satisfy the US authorities that their reason for entering the USA is *not* to take a job. Only then will an entry visa will be issued. Tourists, diplomats and transit travellers all have legitimate business within the country, but may not work within the US job market. If you aren't entering the USA on compassionate grounds and you intend to work then you need to provide proof that you should be considered an exception to the general rule, as provided for by the Immigration and Naturalization Act, Section 212(a)(14). *Don't despair!* Exceptions are many and are provided for. You just have to prove that you fit the criteria.

Aliens (that's officialese for 'foreigners') seeking permission to enter the USA to take up skilled (or unskilled) jobs need first to obtain a verification from the Department of Labor that there aren't sufficient US citizens (or permanent residents whom the US regards as trainee citizens) who are able, willing, qualified and available to do the work the alien proposes to do, *and* that if an alien takes such a job it won't adversely affect the working conditions of persons similarly employed within the USA already (that is, you're not there to break a legal strike or to force down contracted rates of pay).

As you can imagine no single applicant can possibly do such a thing. However, companies actively recruiting overseas can make such a case to the US authorities on behalf of someone they want. If companies have made a conscientious effort to hire within the USA to no avail, then looking for someone overseas is not taking a job from an American, and may positively influence the job market by enabling other Americans to operate more effectively as vacancies are filled.

Now this all seems straightforward. However, if a US college, for instance, is trying to attract a specific person from overseas the job description might be so tightly drawn, tailor-made in fact, to fit no possible US applicant (eg 'must have engaged in at least 10 years full-time field work within the British Isles, speak and read English and Welsh, and have a proven track record in teaching Welsh medieval history'). It might be necessary to justify very carefully why such a specific set of criteria are deemed necessary, especially if the US Department of Labor knows there's actually a glut of good medieval history teachers and researchers already in the USA. But mostly US employers only headhunt overseas for specific skills to complement existing ones, or to bring in someone so prestigious no one is going to be able to object to a brain-drain so obviously to the advantage of the USA.

JOB HUNTING

Jobs as a result of specific advertisements have the advantage of someone in your corner to prepare the paperwork demanded by the US authorities. Removal expenses and help with finding a house and car may be available too (if only on a semi-informal basis).

Once the job's accepted, though, there's little or no choice as to which part of the country you'll have to live in. Having no job to go to does at least enable you to consider a wide range of possible places. Nevertheless a bird in the hand remains better than two in the bush.

An extended visit if you have no job arranged could enable you to see not just a particular city, but to check out feasible commuting. Freeways may imply swift movement between, say downtown Washington DC and central Baltimore, but rush-hour traffic may in practice suggest otherwise. Riding the buses may show how slow public transport really is unless you can live and work near an express route (or a stop on the underground if you are considering one of the few cities to have one).

An extended visit can be used to:

- check out whether or not an area appeals
- whether housing costs are appropriate
- check out schools, public and private.

Think of a particular place in terms of why you are considering the USA:

- Can your love of the Rockies be met by living in Boston?
- Could you afford to ski if you lived in New Orleans?
- You may love New York City's television, but could you live with only three stations in the mountains of North Carolina?
- You may relish the cultural diversity of the USA but what if you were to find yourself stuck in an all-white, Bible-belt town on the one hand or the racial battlefield of the South Bronx on the other?

It's very risky going to the USA for the first time *after* arranging a job. Ideally a month is needed to get the feel of the country, including at least a week at the proposed job location and a week in the surrounding area. A car is essential for getting about except perhaps in New York City, Washington DC and San Francisco. If you want to visit the suburbs away from public transport routes a car is still essential.

Job hunting is hard enough at the best of times. Trying to do it at a distance can be next to impossible.

- A reconnaissance trip to start with can pay off handsomely if only to get you a toe in the water.
- A *lot* of letters will have to be written. This is true in the UK, and it's going to involve a far higher failure rate doing it from overseas, so you'll need to send off that many more enquiries.
- You'll need as large a source of names and addresses as possible. This book can only hope to start you off. You'll need to do considerable detective work in your own field to dig out more.

The rest of this section takes a look at some of the careers and fields of employment within the US economy today, with some general words of advice, and addresses. For the current US phone number ask British Telecom for International Directory Enquiries (153 for the USA). If you have a specific address and it sounds as though you would actually make the call they will ask the US operator to search for the number (using the American son of Ma Bell computer, so it shouldn't take too long).

Self-employed business opportunities
The US can provide significant entrepreneurial advantages for the self-employed. But as at home it is going to be very hard work, probably more so:

- US attitudes towards work mean people expect more of you
- you'll be operating in a new set of business and tax laws (often more demanding than in Britain, contrary perhaps to expectations)
- you'll need to adapt to a new and often bewildering set of commercial ethics, and there'll be a whole new set of trading conditions, expectations about delivery dates and lines of credit.

Will it be worth it? Only you can say so. If you make a go of it the profits can be very substantial. But the hectic race has its losers too, and the US has little in the way of a safety net.

A few addresses that may be of interest:

- National Retail Merchants' Association
  100 West 31st Street, New York, NY 10001

- Insurance Information Institute
  110 William Street, New York, NY 10038

- National Association of Realtors
  155 East Superior Street, Chicago, ILL 60611

Silver lining time: Though failure is very harsh in the USA many would maintain that business failure is not necessarily terminal. Being bankrupt is not like having an anti-social disease. Many people start right over again, and are admired for it. Only those who once down are prepared to stay down are really deemed beyond the pale. The sin is not *falling* down, but *staying* down.

Business and office jobs.

As service industries continue to grow in importance and as computerisation seems to create even more jobs (though not usually for those losing the older jobs) periodic shortages of particular skills are often met by overseas recruitment. The quality press often carry advertisements from US firms, or on their behalf by UK-based recruiters. For those chosen the bureaucratic hassles will be minimised and company lawyers will smooth the way providing necessary supporting documentation for any visa application.

For more general information on recruitment it may be worthwhile writing to the following:

- National Association of Public Accountants
  1010 N Fairfax St, Alexandria, VA 22314

- American Bankers' Association
  1120 Connecticut Avenue NW, Washington DC 20036

- United Business Schools Association
  1730 M Street NW, Washington DC 20036

- American Federation of Information Processing Societies
  1899 Preston White Drive, Reston, VA 22091

- National Association of Public Adjusters
  1613 Munsey Building, Baltimore, MD 21202

- Insurance Information Institute
  110 William Street, New York, NY 10038

- National Secretaries Association
  2440 Pershing Road, Suite G-10, Kansas City, MO 64108

Media and the arts

Unless you are an artist of international renown it is very difficult to enter the USA to take part in its world famous communications industry. Artists visiting for concert tours need special arrangements with US Equity to ensure they come under reciprocal agreements arranged with British Equity. Visits and performance tours can and are arranged, not just by impresarios with legal departments to smooth the hassles but by various US agencies. The US Department of the Interior, for instance, arranges international festivals for traditional musicians from overseas.

Some skilled or gifted people enter this field by way of placements as part of their postgraduate degrees at US colleges. Entrance to such courses is, however, competitive, especially where financial assistance is needed, and funds sufficient for the issuing of a non-immigrant student visa must be available *prior* to applying for a visa (see the later section on student visas).

Assuming that you are not wanting to be reunited with family already in the USA, that you are not an anti-communist refugee, that you don't have lots of money to invest, and that you aren't an artist of sufficient renown, you will need to be accepted by a US employer able to prove the post has been unsuccessfully advertised within the USA. This means in practice that only professional people already well established in their careers will be recruited, and so eligible for entry to work.

Remember: Sarah Brightman (Andrew Lloyd Webber's wife) was initially not deemed to be of sufficient renown by US Equity and the INS to appear on Broadway in her husband's show.

If you consider that you are capable of getting the right entry and work permits here are some addresses you may find helpful:

- Society of Illustrators
  128 East 63rd Street, New York, NY 10021

- Professional Photographers of America Inc
  1090 Executive Way, Oakleaf Common, Des Plaines, Illinois 60018

- Photo Marketing Association
  603 Lansing Avenue, Jackson, Michigan 49202

- Printing Industries of America
  1730 North Wynn Street, Arlington, Virginia 22201

- Society For Technical Communications Inc
  Suite 421, 1010 Vermont Ave NW, Washington DC 20005

- National Association of Broadcasters
  1771 North Street NW, Washington DC 20036

- Federal Communications Commission
  1919 M Street NW, Washington DC 20554

- US Equity (Actors' Equity Association)
  165 West 46th Street, New York, NY 10036

For those with electrical/electronic skills:

- Communication Workers of America
  1925 K Street NW, Washington DC 20006

Education, caring and social services
A desire to get rich quickly will not propel you into this line of work. Also, such public jobs depend heavily upon government spending programmes as so many are directly tied to Federal programmes (and so Federal budgets). With money (outside the military budget) increasingly tight the job situation is not rosy. Furthermore many jobs will require US qualifications to work in the USA.

Many people from overseas will only enter these fields if eligible for residence on other grounds. Once within the US job market, however, foreign professionals may be able to gain credit for courses overseas, or must be prepared to enter related jobs, such as legal paraprofessionals, library technicians or teachers' aides.

Some useful addresses:

- Legal Paraprofessional, American Bar Association
  1155 East 60th Street, Chicago, Illinois 60637

- Council of Library Science
  University of Mississippi, University, Mississippi 38677

- National Recreation and Parks Association
  1601 North Kent Street, Arlington, Virginia 22209

- National Education Association
  1201 16th Street NW, Washington DC 20036

Engineering and science
Jobs are very competitive, so looking for a US job in these fields means looking for US firms that are actively recruiting overseas. Professional journals and magazines which carry such recruitment advertisements can be found in large public and polytechnics or university libraries — see their current acquisitions section (ask at main desk, and don't worry:

members of the general public are usually welcome to use such specialised materials).

US recruitment agencies will also pinpoint their efforts upon certain areas of the country. If an aerospace firm closes down US firms hoping to attract away skilled labour will advertise locally, even open local recruitment offices. Of course it is the most modern skills they seek, held by people with at least 20 years work left in them. The industrial cities of the USA already have far too many people of their own approaching their fifties with skills no longer needed anywhere.

A few addresses that might be useful.

- American Institute of Aeronautics and Astronautics
  1290 Avenue of the Americas, New York, NY 10019

- American Society for Agricultural Engineers
  2950 Niles Road, St Joseph, Michigan 49085

- Air Conditioning and Refrigeration Institute
  1815 North Fort Myers Drive, Arlington, Virginia 22209

- US Energy Information Administration
  1000 Independence Ave NW, Washington DC 20585

- American Institute of Biological Sciences
  1401 Wilson Boulevard, Arlington, Virginia 22209

- American Institute of Chemical Engineers
  345 East 47th Street, New York, NY 10017

- American Society of Civil Engineers
  345 East 47th Street, New York, NY 10017

- Institute of Electrical and Electronic Engineers
  345 East 47th Street, New York, NY 10017

- Institute of Food Technologists
  Suite 2120, 221 North LaSalle Street, Chicago, Ill 60601

- Society of American Foresters
  1010 16th Street NW, Washington DC 20036

- American Geological Institute
  52025 Leesburg Pike, Falls Church, Virginia 22041

- American Institute for Industrial Engineering
  25 Technology Park, Norcross, Atlanta, Georgia 30071

- Instrumentation Society of America
  400 Stanwix Street, Pittsburgh, Pennsylvania 15222

- Marine Technology Society
  1730 M Street NW, Washington DC 20036

- American Society of Mechanical Engineers
  345 East 47th Street, New York, NY 10017

- American Meteorological Society
  45 Beacon Street, Boston, Massachusetts 02108

- American Congress on Surveying and Mapping
  Woodward Building, 733 15th Street NW, Washington DC 20005

- American Institute for Design and Drafting
  3119 Prince Road, Bartlesville, Oklahoma 74003

Health care services

The shortage of doctors and nurses has significantly increased the need for technicians who can take over routine health care duties such as blood tests and dispensing medicines. The bureaucracy necessary to operate the complex private and public health care programmes, plus the growing number of older people, adds up to more health care jobs at many levels.

Once within the health care profession this is a career field that offers good salaries and good conditions. Health jobs offer steady work with few lay offs, as well as health care benefits, a most useful perk in a country where the high cost of health insurance can be a major drawback.

Most medical jobs require US training, but due to the pressures upon administrators to find suitably trained people it may be possible to gain significant credit for professional qualifications gained from recognised establishments overseas. Doctors, for instance, can take special exams to ensure that they are trained to a US level.

Some useful addresses:

- American Dental Assistants Association
  211 Chicago Drive, Chicago, Ill 60611

- American Dental Hygienists Association
  211 East Chicago Ave, Chicago, Ill 60611

- American Hospital Association
  840 North Lake Drive, Chicago, Ill 60611

- Emergency Medical Service Branch
  National Highway Traffic Safety Administration
  400 7th Street SW, Washington DC 20590

- American Association of Medical Assistants
  1 East Walker Drive, Suite 1510, Chicago, Ill 60601

- American Society for Medical Technology
  5555 West Loop South, Bellaire, Texas 77401

- American Medical Record Association
  John Hancock Center, Suite 1850, 875 North Michigan Avenue,
  Chicago, Ill 60611

- National Association for Practical Nurse Education & Service
  122 East 42nd Street, Suite 800, New York, NY 10017

- American Nurses' Association
  2420 Pershing Road, Kansas City, Missouri 64108

- American Occupational Therapy Association
  6000 Executive Boulevard, Rockville, Maryland 20852

- Association of Operating-Room Technicians
  110 West Littleton Boulevard, Suite 201, Littleton, Colorado 80120

- National Academy of Opticianry
  514 Chestnut Street, Big Rapids, Michigan 49307

- American Optometric Association
  7000 Chippewa Street, St Louis, Missouri 63119

- American Physical Therapy Association
  1156 15th Street NW, Washington DC 20005

- American Society of Radiologic Technologists
  645 North Michigan Avenue, Chicago, Ill 60611

- American Association for Respiratory Therapy
  7411 Hines Place, Dallas, Texas 75235

Recruitment drives are held from time to time in the UK, and are accompanied by considerable media interest, so opportunities may present themselves to anyone ready and willing to relocate. But beware: US salaries may seem very high, but if you couldn't afford to move from Birmingham to London because of the high cost of living in the southeast you may not be able to afford housing in New York City either. But a move from London to rural Minnesota might be very profitable.

Any move by a single person to the USA (if only for a year or so) may be worthwhile just for the experience. And of course many single people going over to work in the USA also marry in America, whatever their original plans.

Service industries

As people have more money and more leisure time service industries, particularly those dealing directly with the general public, grow and grow in number and importance. Many service jobs, though, are poorly paid, recruiting non-unionised teenagers, as in fast-food outlets. These jobs may be available on a casual basis, but are not career jobs, nor are such jobs available for foreigners without resident status. However, some services do require specialist skills, such as the rescue and police services. Unfortunately such public services are often geared to government spending levels. In certain parts of New York City public services have been subject to 'planned shrinkage'!   If you have already served in the fire service contact:

● International Association of Firefighters
  1750 New York Avenue NW, Washington DC 20006

For information on police opportunities write to the state police department of any State you are interested in, which will probably be located in the State capital (eg Albany for New York, Tallahessee for Florida, or Sacramento for California). There is no federal police force (unlike the Mounties in Canada) as law and order is very much a State responsibility (as it remains for each country in the European Community, with which the USA should perhaps be more properly compared). Alan Whicker presented a British police officer's view of both the service and his Los Angeles 'beat' on his 1986 television series (see *Whicker's New World,* available from Book Club Associates at considerable savings on the £11 hardback price).

Transport

Employment is expected to increase for highway and air jobs, but continues to decline for railway work. Sales and reservation jobs are now much like any other job that deals directly with the general public within catering or tourism. Most jobs are therefore only available for those already US residents. Aircraft mechanics need a licence from a Federal Aviation Administration (FAA) approved school, plus con-

---

A note of warning: if you are thinking of investing money, time or effort in any commercial trucking enterprise, please get professional advice. Moving furniture in a VW bus for friends or acquaintances is one thing, but getting into long haul trucking may soon bring you up against the International Teamsters (at best) or the Mafia (at worst). Neither organisation tends to encourage people moving onto their turf.

siderable experience, usually gained in the US military. Except for overseas applicants with highly unusual skills this field is essentially closed to people who don't already have US residence.

Contract work
Contract work is advertised in the UK press, primarily as available for engineering and electronics persons, ranging from a few months to a couple of years. Employment is on US terms (with minimal holidays) but at very good rates of pay even by US standards. Fixed terms are usually necessary for immigration regulation purposes. Beyond the end of the contract there is no security, and you will have to have one eye always on the next contract opportunity, which may mar the travel time between contracts. It'll play havoc with family life.

Let's consider the pros and cons:

Good news
- Good pay
- experience of USA
- formalities undertaken by employer
- fares paid
- nomadic
- travel between contracts

Bad news
- fixed term
- you may not be able to stay on
- can't change employer
- can't visit beforehand
- hard on family life
- you may be reluctant to spend money if no further job is in sight

APPLYING FOR A JOB

Applying for any job, especially one overseas, demands great care. You are presenting yourself, so take your time. You only get one bite of the apple. Show your draft copy to someone, whether a careers adviser, a relative in business, or just a friend. Their comments may be all the feedback you'll get, and so may be invaluable.

How well you fill in an application form is generally crucial: it is usually the first contact with an employer. The overall impression created by a completed form will precede you to any further interview. In the competitive job market today, the importance of well presented and well thought out applications *cannot be over-emphasised.*

The job hunters perspective

From the job seeker's perspective application forms are a huge hurdle. You generally have to complete a great many just to get one interview; it can be very time consuming; and they often ask the most awkward and difficult questions. But there is no escape from them if you hope to find a job.

Think of applications as a challenge — a means of presenting as positive and interesting (but truthful) picture of yourself as you can. Make sure the employer will want to find out more about you.

The employer's perspective

From the employer's point of view application forms are vital selection documents. Most employers cannot interview all applicants, so half or more are usually eliminated through this initial screening. Application forms provide an economical basis for deciding which candidates are most likely to meet their criteria. Their decisions will be based not only on what you write, but also on *how you present it.*

Presenting your application form

The effectiveness of your application will depend largely upon your prior preparation. You cannot expect to sit down 'cold' with any application form and do justice to yourself there and then. Prior work is essential.

Assess yourself

Many questions will focus on you as a person:

- What have you gained from your education/training/career so far?
- Why do you think you would make a useful member of their firm?
- What are your main strengths and weaknesses?

Thorough self-analysis and relating your skills, interests and background to the demands of the job are vital steps in the application process, enabling you to present a convincing case for yourself.

Research

Research the job and the particular employer before filling in the forms. You need to find out as much as you can about both the organisation and the job. Lack of such homework is almost always evident and a common basis for rejection at this stage.

Types of questions

Although forms vary, and range from one side of foolscap concentrating on factual information, to booklets requiring almost a total life history, they usually ask for the following information:

Personal details and educational background
Make sure all the information is accurate and nothing **relevant** has been omitted. It is usually best not to list failures unless specifically asked to do so or unless they indicate a gap in your life that cannot otherwise be accounted for. Try, however, to be positive wherever possible. If you feel you must say how far you fell make sure they know how soon you came back up to try again and to succeed.

Interests, extra-curricular activities and positions of responsibility
Selectors will deduce quite a lot from what you do (or do not do) with your spare time. They will particularly interested in positions of responsibility and evidence of initiatives. This is particularly crucial when applying for your first ever job (when you cannot offer practical experience). Do you seem to be an active, social type or more of a loner? Are you a single-minded specialist or an all rounder? Is there evidence of leadership abilities, of being able to work well in a team? The main thing is to try and write positively about your activities — whatever they may be.

Work experience/previous jobs
Employers are interested in any work experience you have had. When describing your employment include a brief description of the duties involved. Try and demonstrate what you gained from this experience, such as working under pressure, with the general public, out of doors, shift work, etc. Particularly if you are applying for your first job do not leave anything out. Anything and everything can count as useful experience.

If you are further along with your career you can be more choosey. Even here, though, vacation work twenty years ago might be worth mentioning, if for instance it was in the USA (and so the company knows that early on you showed initiative, and that you have already had some experience of living in the USA).

Job choice/career aspirations
Almost all application forms will have some questions aimed at drawing out your motivation for the particular job, and for determining your longer term career aspirations. It is vital that you communicate interest in the job and the organisation, backed up by whatever concrete evidence you can use.

Knowing precisely what the company has to offer is crucial (you *must* read the recruitment literature carefully). Relate your needs, interests and aspirations to what they say they need. Indicate what specific factors have influenced your career choice and why you think your combination of experience, qualifications and personal attributes are appropriate for the job in question.

Open-ended questions
These can include:

- What have been your main achievements in life?
- What initiatives have you taken and what have you been able to accomplish?
- What difficulties and disappointments have you met and how have you tackled them?

Such questions may seem very intimidating at first, particularly since most of us have had relatively ordinary careers, unpunctuated by momentous accomplishments, events or turning points. However difficult such questions may seem, try to see them as an opportunity to portray something interesting and positive about yourself and to demonstrate your ability to communicate clearly and concisely.

Employers are generally more concerned with what an experience meant to you personally, how you dealt with it, or what you gained from it, than the actual event itself. Thus, persevering with months of boring assembly line work rather than going on the dole could be more relevant than going to climb Mt Everest (if for example you were killing time before going to take a business management course).

It is useful to think about what the employer is trying to get at by asking this type of question. There is no standard or correct answer. You need to write about your own experiences!

Additional information
Many forms have a space for anything additional you feel you could usefully tell them. There may be something you thought they would want to know but don't seem to have asked for. Perhaps you could mention foreign travel, expeditions, or special qualifications that might suggest the sort of person you are. Maybe you could use this opportunity to explain why you were made redundant. You may be able to write something distinctive that will make you stand out from the general run of the mill applicant. If your area of responsibility was increasingly profitable but was undermined by an asset-stripping take-over then say so. You may get no other chance to explain why you are looking for work.

Questions to be raised at interview
This gives the interviewer advance notice of questions you might want to ask and gives the selector a further opportunity to assess the quality of

your thinking about the job. Never leave this section blank. And never ask just about salary and holiday matters. Think carefully about what you have read in the company literature. Are there gaps in what they have said about the company? Perhaps you still feel you need to know about the range of training they will provide? The likeliness of career progression? Do not be afraid to ask challenging questions.

Referees

If you have recently completed formal education one of these should be an academic referee. The second should be a previous employer or someone (not a relative) who knows your career well, and can comment upon your performance, particularly if it is not possible to ask your present employer for a reference (if you don't want it to be known that you are applying for jobs elsewhere). *Always* consult referees *before* naming them, and make sure that they have a good idea about what you are applying for.

General guidelines

- Try to approach the firm as *positively* as possible. It is important to be truthful, but you will have to **sell yourself** and convince the employer that you really want the job and have the ability and potential to succeed at it. Don't make claims you cannot substantiate, but remember, no points are given for modesty.
- Do all the necessary preparation – **assess** yourself, **research** the job and the company and **relate** your attributes and aspirations to the demands of the job.
- Before writing anything, read the form carefully to get the feel of what to put where and how much space you have.
- Follow all the instructions carefully – mistakes will be interpreted as an indication of carelessness.
- **Make a draft version of what you intend to write.** This can be done on a photocopy of the application form. It is particularly important to draft out answers to open-ended questions and, ideally, to put the draft away for a day or so before returning to it with a fresh eye.
- Use black ink (many photocopies may have to be taken).
- Pay particular attention to neatness and spelling. Selectors will not be well disposed to applications that are untidy, difficult to read, or filled with spelling errors. Type, unless specifically asked to write in your own hand.
- Make sure the layout is clear and attractive. First impressions are important.
- Do not leave any unexplained chronological gaps.
- Answer *all* the questions, unless not applicable.

- Relate what you write to the precise requirements of the job.
- Always keep a photocopy of completed applications. They will be necessary at the interview stage (you'll need to see what you told them beforehand!).
- Many of the questions asked at interviews will be based on answers you have provided on the form. Before an interview it is vital to think about how your responses might be further developed.
- If you need help, ask a friend or colleague. They can help you think through the difficult questions and can advise on the overall impact your application makes.

Curriculum vitae (CV)
Some very detailed application forms (similar to those for university entrance) do not require a separate CV, but with most applications you should send one along. Known as a **resumé** in the USA it is a personal statement of:

- Who you are
- What you have done already
- What qualifications you have
- What you have to offer

- It should be set out in a generally acceptable format, be typed, and carefully spaced so that the layout draws the reader's attention to essential information in a methodological and logical fashion. The usual format is as follows:

Personal	Nationality, age, date of birth (spelled out in full), marital status, address, telephone numbers (work and home), relevant extra information (hobbies, association membership).
Employment	Names and addresses of past employers, dates of employment, positions and responsibilities held, with reasons for leaving.
Education	Dates and schools, colleges, universities attended, examinations passed (with dates and grades), with any other qualifications

- It's usual to set out present positions first and then work back. If a column for dates is kept clearly visible on the left this should be quite clear to any reader.
- If you have little or not employment to record (if straight from college) place the education section *before* the employment section.

- If you are sending out multiple applications use the best copier you can afford. It may be worthwhile to visit a copyshop rather than rely upon doing it yourself in a coin-in-the-slot machine. For isolated applications send an original rather than a copy.

Remember: US students have long typed all their work so the quality of your competition's CVs will be very high. If in doubt pay for your CV to be professionally typed and copied.

Sending off applications

- **Type** your covering letter on good quality A4 paper, and send it in an appropriately sized envelop with your CV. Neatly type the envelope using the correct zip code. It is usual in the USA to place your address in the upper left hand corner of the addressed side of the envelop. Use the correct value stamp and an airmail sticker. The use of a commemorative stamp on a well produced envelope may well catch someone's eye in a pile of applications.
- If you wish for confirmation of receipt of your application, or wish for items to be returned, or further information to be forwarded, always send either sufficient postage stamps (saved from last year's Florida holiday or bought from a stamp dealer!) or sufficient International Reply Coupons (available at your post office).

Offered a job?

Before accepting any job abroad make absolutely certain you are aware of all relevant factors:

- Are your professional qualifications acceptable in their existing form in the USA?
- Who will be responsible for getting the appropriate papers, yourself or the employer?
- What is the length of the contract? Is there a probationary period?
- What is the salary and when will the first payment be made, and in what form?
- Who is responsible for deductions?
- What vacation entitlements are there in the first year?
- What relocation help is available? If so, when and how much?
- What accommodation arrangements are there, for how long and at what cost?
- Will commuting be necessary? Is public transport feasible?
- What sickness provision is there for self and for family? When does it take effect?
- What pre-conditions exist? Will you be asked to sit any in-house examinations, undergo medical tests?

If you are offered a job it may well be necessary to accept or reject it quite quickly. The more versed you are in the problems of moving the easier it will be to concentrate upon the essential factors upon which you'll make your decision. Further help and preparation can be gained from reading Harry Brown's *Working Abroad?*, published in Plymouth by Northcote House in 1986. This covers in more detail all the issues raised here, particularly secondments, and the implications for the whole family. There is also a Daily Telegraph guide by Godfrey Golzen also called *Working Abroad,* published by Kogan Page in 1987 for £6.95, which details the problems of living and working overseas, with general and country-specific material.

COMMUTING AS AN OPTION

Rather than change countries it may be easier to commute between Britain and the US. Academics, journalists and certain businessmen may find living in both countries feasible.

Points to consider:

- costs of maintaining two bases
- costs of air fares
- time involved in travelling
- tax liability
- immigration standing

All these points need careful consideration, else you could find yourself committed to far more travel and far greater costs than initially anticipated.

Two bases
There are several options worth thinking about:

- **Home in UK and staying with US friends**
  You can't stay too long, or you'll outlive your welcome. Paying for a spare room may solve this problem. You'll avoid US local taxes and the problem of leaving your US base unoccupied (and thus vulnerable) for long periods.

- **Home in the UK and own place in US**
  If this involves owning in the UK and renting in the US you may get tax advantages from your UK home as your 'principal residence' and the rented flat as a business expense. This is easier than the other way around, as it leaves a Briton with an existing relationship with the Inland Revenue. Avoid starting any relationship with the

more strict Internal Revenue Service in the USA. Better the devil you know...

- **Base in the UK, with long-stay hotel accommodation in the USA**
  This could be right for you, but only if you intend to stay put, say in New York City or Los Angeles. Otherwise you'll be humping stuff around the US. But for a month or so long-stay rates can be attractive, being much lower than daily rates. At worst you could try staying at a basic level at the YMCA or YWCA, though security for business materials while you're out at work might be worrying. A halfway solution might be to rent an efficiency room from a motel, which would include a kitchen besides the usual facilities.

Cost of air fares

If you are self-employed these costs can start to eat into profits, even if you are able to claim them as business expenses for tax purposes.

You may well not want to wait for cheaper standby places, nor can you travel to and fro wedged into a tourist seat too frequently. Eventually you'll need to travel at some expense if only to get some sleep and to minimise jet lag. Concorde back from Washington DC or New York City is ideal, but pricey.

What other costs would be involved?

- getting to and from the airport
- long-stay car parks
- shipping over goods and materials.

Travel times

Few will live in the lea of Heathrow or Gatwick nor will a US base necessarily be near to JFK or Newark. The journey from Birmingham to Heathrow is tortuous with luggage, though easy by motorway. What do you do with the car at Terminal 4? Flying down from Birmingham International may be more convenient, but may raise your travel costs by 20%.

Do you want to have a three hour motorway drive home after arriving at Heathrow from New York City? If you'd flown Concorde then Heathrow would be only half way home!

Tax liability

Though US-UK treaties ensure that you'll only be taxed on the same income once, each country will want it to be in their system. The rule of thumb is that you'll be taxed in the country where you spend most of your time. The United States IRS uses a complicated formula to calculate a notional definition of where you live, or as bureaucrats prefer to put it: where you have a 'substantial preference'! (*see* p.146)

If there's any doubt where you live then both bureaucracies will read their own regulations to their own fiscal advantage (wouldn't you?), may change the rules from year to year, and may redefine what is meant by a permanent base, the indicator of where you intend to be taxed.

If at all possible keep your residency status the same from year to year, so that you only have to deal with one pack of wolves at a time (remember the military nightmare of a war on two fronts).

For the US view of tax details and so forth see the IRS booklet No 518 *Foreign Workers, Scholars and Exchange Visitors*.

For an unofficial but authoritative British view see *The Expatriate's Guide* by Andrew Burgess, an ex-Inland Revenue officer now the director of financial planning at Neville Russell Accountants, from whom it can be obtained for £2.50 including post and packing. Write to 246 Bishopgate, London WC2 ((01) 377 1000). This is a most useful guide for those interested in the tax consequences of living and working in the USA. As a guide it is well thought out, with good headings and an index to help you find your way through the issues.

Immigration standing
US regulations assume that you are either a visitor or an immigrant. Exceptions get very messy and confused. Many people, afraid of falling between two stools, hire a lawyer specialising in immigration matters, though this can be expensive, and is no guarantee of a satisfactory outcome, especially if the lawyer is mainly used to dealing with people who want to get permanent residency status. Most people would get by with the normal commercial non-resident B1 visa. Academics, for instance, usually get the B1-2 visa valid for multiple entry that would allow visits and commercial trips. This is because they would be working for UK-based employers (colleges and publishers).

If you want to work for a US-based employer you will need an employment visa or residency status (the famous so-called *Green* Card). This is much harder to get of course, unless you can arrange to be hired by, and paid by, the UK subsidiary (or even a UK parent company).

'Substantial preference'

In theory it's quite simple:

> 31 days in the USA this calendar year *and* 183 days in this year *plus* the last 2 years, but counting only a third of last year's days, and counting only an eighth of the previous year's.

Got it?

A worked example:

In 1987 you spent 100 days in the USA and these are counted in full	100
1986 is the previous year, of which 100 again were spent in the USA *but* only a third count	$33\frac{1}{3}$
Plus 80 days for 1985, where only an eighth count	10
	$143\frac{1}{3}$

So, though you spent more than 31 days in the USA in 1987, you stayed only $143\frac{1}{3}$ in 1985-7 rather than the 183 that would have made you liable for US tax.

Easy, isn't it!

INVESTING IN THE USA

For people with more than their lives and families to invest in the USA investment may or may not involve actually moving to the USA. Either way it needs expert advice. Selling your thriving fish and chip shop here, packing the money into a suitcase and going through US customs and immigration as a tourist (it's been done) is not advisable. There are too many tales of people coming sadly and very badly unstuck, investing in motels that then go bust as the new freeway opens and takes all the passing trade elsewhere (haven't they seen *Psycho* or *The Postman Always Rings Twice?*). Don't buy a college town bar just as the State's liquor laws change to stop students under 21 drinking. Too many small investors end up washing floors, dishes and windows, one-step ahead of the Immigration and Naturalization Service (INS), not to mention the Teamsters or the Mafia if they think you are muscling in on their patch.

For more specific and detailed information see the appropriate *Daily Telegraph* Guide by Peter Farrell *How to Buy a Business,* published by

Kogan Page of London in 1983. Though certain specifics may age the general approach necessary to such a major transaction surely doesn't.

It might be wise at this point to draw your attention to another vital guide also published by Kogan Page: Paul Chaplin's *Choosing and Using Professional Advisers.* A second edition came out in 1986.

If property investment is proposed an essential work of reference is Nigel A Eastway and David Young's *Expatriate Tax and Investment Guide,* published in London by Longman in 1985 (hardback at £12.50). Besides dealing with the joys of double taxation, capital gains and capital transfer taxes, this otherwise general source of information specifically presents a section tailored to the needs of those people with an eye on the United States.

For the manufacturer who wants to explore the possibilities of investing in a sales campaign within the USA the British Overseas Trade Board should be approached. Their address is:

- BOTB, Ladywood House, Stephenson Street, Birmingham, B2 4DH ((021) 632 4111).

They provide seed corn grants for market research, and can provide help with stands at trade fairs overseas. They do, however, tend to insist that suppliers seeking to penetrate the US market do so from a tested and tried basis within local and European markets. The US market should be approached from strength rather than speculatively.

Using a US-based trading company
The entrepreneur who sees the US market as impenetrable except from within may well be missing an equally appropriate option. For those with no wish to leave home for more than the occasional and very necessary business trip the very thought of emigration may so repel that any further interest in the US market may die as well.

But markets overseas are ever more critical. The more specialist the product the more commercially necessary will it be to sell it within the USA. Lacking the knowledge of international corporations and the financial ability to buy it in (as would a larger concern), the small entrepreneur may consider the US market as inaccessible as a weekend climber finds Mt Everest. What is needed is a proven, low-cost guide for the small entrepreneur into this potentially most lucrative markets. 'Trading posts' now provide such a guide.

The US economy continues to suck in not only consumer and electronic goods from overseas, but increasingly seeks foreign ideas, techniques and materials. Research and development (R & D) concerns servicing the space, semiconductor and electronics industries are looking not just for British experts to move to the USA but also to buy, license or even fund those techniques deemed essential if the USA is to survive its huge trade deficit.

One such establishment geared up to making the crucial link between the specialist US market and the British entrepreneur is Microscience Inc, the specialist instrumentation consultancy firm of Tony Drybanski, himself a British expatriate. With offices on both coasts, in the Boston area near Route 128 (and hence via Interstate 95 to the whole Atlantic east coast) and in Silicon Valley California for the growing Pacific west coast, firms like Microscience Inc provide a more specialist marketing service than has previously been available.

This new generation of intermediaries is more active on behalf of customers, rather than just computer clearing house. Matching products with R & D customers, trading firms actively join suppliers in selling their product to the market, coupled with overseeing the actual processes of importing, distribution and after-sales support. A specialist staff would handle all sales and marketing in return for exclusive distribution rights. The trading company buys only from suppliers whose product reliability is excellent. The trading company then sells to US end users with suitable credit ratings. Trading companies thus act as a risk-taking buffer between the supplier and the buyer, profiting not on a commission basis, but on the difference between their buying and selling prices.

So successful has this procedure been that US blue chip customers such as Bell, Exxon, Hewlett Packard, IBM, MIT, NASA and Texas Instruments now provide Microscience Inc with lists of sought products. The management approach is to focus upon universities, government and corporate research rather than geographical regions (the latter being more appropriate for consumer rather than technological products). The time scale is extended to ensure both products and suppliers are carefully chosen, with an overt emphasis upon sound and proven technology, strong management, and a whole-hearted commitment to both the product and the customer.

The objective of Microscience Inc is over $1 million in sales per company. To ensure this companies need to be able to fund a high entry cost, up to $250,000. But to place a qualified and committed company representative over in the USA could cost over half this sum, with no local backup: an expensive way to send rarely effective brochures that could have gone in the post, if not straight in the bin. Their address is: 182 Forbes Road, Braintree, Mass. 02184 (010-1- (617) 849 1952).

This massive initial cost will of course exclude most UK companies from even considering going it alone, never mind in tandem with a trading company. Other options do exist:

- the brochure blitz
- the phone call campaign
- the personal contact
- the transatlantic trip
- buying in skills from local polytechnics and universities
- cooperation with bodies actively promoting US investment in the UK, such as the **Staffordshire Development Association,** PO Box 11, Martin Street, Stafford ST16 2LH ((0785) 223121)
- cooperation with agencies promoting British exports in the USA, such as the **British Overseas Trade Board,** Chantry House, High Street, Coleshill B46 3BP ((0675) 62577)

Further reading

There is a regular small business column in the financial section of the *Guardian.* General business climate and conditions in the USA are increasingly important in the weekly *Economist* (as an ever larger proportion of its readership is American). There is always of course *The Financial Times.* Knowing your way around the FT makes going through back copies much easier for large parts can safely be ignored so long as relevant sections are carefully monitored.

Some contact numbers:

- British Overseas Trade Board   (021) 632 4111
- US International Marketing Center   (01) 629 4304
- US Regional Export Development Office   (01) 629 1461
- American Chamber of Commerce (UK)   (01) 493 0381
- US Embassy Commercial Reference Library (01) 499 9000, ext. 2026
- United States Information Service (USIS)   (01) 499 9000, ext. 2020
- West Midlands Industrial Development Association   (0675) 62577

9
Money Matters

CASH

Payment is generally made with cash despite the widespread use of credit cards, charge cards, personal cheques (checks) and travellers' cheques. Beware:

- All US banknotes (bills) are **green,** the same size, and have similar layouts (though a different president's face appears on each denomination).
- You may come across the following sign: 'Legal tender not accepted'. It means just what it says. Payment is by prepaid token or by card (credit or charge). It's all part of the war against crime: no cash means there's nothing to steal.

PERSONAL CHEQUES

Personal cheques are far less convenient than in the UK. They are subject to more scrutiny and more delay than you have ever met before, and can usually only be used locally within the area served by your bank. Unfortunately your bank may well turn out to be far more local than you might have expected from its name as 'First National Bank of...'.

To use a cheque it must be overprinted with your name, address, telephone number, account number, and in some places your driver's licence number. *And* you'll need local identification (ID).

What's ID?
This usually means a driving licence at the very least. It'll be asked for whenever you use any form of cheque, even travellers' cheques! Don't bother trying to explain to the clerk that travellers' cheques are as good as cash if signed at time of use. You'll be shown the sign that hangs everywhere 'All checks must have ID'.

Once, in the Smithsonian Institute bookshop in Washington DC, an American Express dollar travellers' cheque was refused with reference to just such a sign (since taken down), and the clerk wanted *local* identification. The cheque wasn't accepted until a five year old, almost expired, US government ID was produced (relic of a previous spell working in the capital).

The reason cheques cause so much hassle is quite simple. Cheque theft is endemic. Furthermore, if you leave a retailer with a cheque that bounces (and there are no guarantee cards to ensure payment up to a certain level) they'll want to find you to recover the value of the cheque, plus their administrative costs, plus the penalty payment the bank charged them. You may see signs warning you that a bounced cheque will cost you $5. As current accounts cannot go into the red the possibilities of going into cheque bouncing territory is high if you'd been used to the more casual situation in Britain.

CREDIT CARDS

Credit cards are more widely used than in Germany, but, surprisingly not as widely as in the UK. Most stores and petrol stations will accept VISA or Access ('Mastercharge') but there are still enough places that won't accept either card to make things tricky if you run out of petrol or need accommodation in out of the way places. Check beforehand if you can. Also, you may have to pay a surcharge for using a credit card.

Don't be surprised if the clerk hands you back not just the credit slip top copy but also the carbon. A few years back there was a rash of carbon-based frauds. Retrieving used carbons from bins gave thieves customers' credit card numbers, which were then used to order goods by telephone. Many people now expect to be offered the carbon for disposal.

Creditworthiness

Creditworthiness is different from what you're used to. It is *illegal* in many states to go unexpectedly overdrawn. If the bank were to honour your cheque it would be giving you its own money, so you would have spent what doesn't belong to you. If, on the other hand, the bank won't honour your cheque you have just attempted to defraud the retailer stuck with the bouncing cheque. Either way you are deemed to be beyond the pale. And your creditworthiness will disappear, which may hurt you when it comes to buying a car, or just trying to obtain a credit card.

Credit card companies require an indication you won't do a bunk and disappear after a shopping spree, so they may check your bank, your employer and commercially available bad-debts lists. If you are self-employed and live in a trailer then credit won't be available.

BANKS

Banks are organised somewhat differently than in Britain, and this affects how they operate and the services they provide. *Don't deposit any money in an uninsured bank.* Many lived to regret doing just that in the 1930s Great Depression. The Federal government set up the Federal Deposit Insurance Corporation (FDIC) to guarantee deposits (and so minimising the chance that there would ever be a dangerous loss of confidence in the financial system among small to medium savers). The maximum insured individual deposit continuously rises. By the mid 1980s it had reached $100,000 (more than most of us will ever have in the bank!).

SAVINGS AND LOAN ASSOCIATIONS

Savings and loan associations are the nearest equivalent to British building societies. Loans are generally fixed interest (good if you finance a property when the rates are low, not so good if they were very high), though loans are often refinanced if rates change substantially, or if house prices rise so high you are undermortgaged and so find you can raise more money on the property (say for an extension, a pool or even to go back to college). If depositing make sure the association is insured by the savings and loan version of the FDIC (the Federal Savings and Loan Insurance Corporation (FSLIC).

PENSION PLANS

Pension plans depend upon how long you intend to stay in the USA. If you are going to return home in a year or so you may just have to accept that all your required pension payments will be for nought. If your company can transfer them all well and good. If you leave the USA with all taxes paid you may be able to claim your US social security payments back, but only if you can show that you have taken no deductions, have paid tax at the flat rate, and will not be returning to the US to live. Students on an F visa may be able to do this, but it may well be cheaper for long-term visitors to pay as little tax as possible and to pay their social security knowing they'll get nothing for it. Students should consult their foreign student office at their university.

For those more affluent visitors who pay both tax and social security a tax accountant may be needed to get the best deal. And if you hear Americans talk about how rapidly support for the IRA is growing remember that in all probability they are referring to **individual retirement accounts** which involve tax-free savings earmarked for retirement. Such accounts enable people to move between jobs with no pension loss (so long as they can keep making the payments).

HEALTH INSURANCE

Health insurance may well be a major fringe benefit of a job offer. Few companies, however, offer full coverage for the employee and the rest of the family. You need to know precisely what the cover includes. Pre-existing conditions will of course be excluded, but beware of ceilings on payments for treatment. Cover will often only be for 80% of costs up to say $10,000, and 100% over that. Pregnancy may not be included, nor will dental and optical charges. Check as to when the cover comes into force — it might not be until 6 months into the job. Ask:

- When does the cover start?
- Who's covered?
- What's included?

It is essential to know what the situation is beforehand so that you can arrange bridging cover before you leave Britain. And you had better get those details in writing in case there's any dispute when push comes to shove. Illness can be emotionally devastating. In the USA it can also destroy the financial security of a family, and often does. Catastrophic illness can destroy the family just as much as the patient. At least be insured!

Medicare: the situation as of 1987
Medicare is the nearest thing the US has to Britain's National Health Service, but it applies only to the aged (not to be confused with **Medicaid**, a joint federal and state health care programme for the poor). Medicare pays hospital bills less certain deductibles for the first 60 days only.

Then the patient has to pay:

- $130 per day for one month.
- then $260 per day for the next two months
- and then *all* the bills from then on.

To cover the gap between what Medicare pays and the bills some people will have taken out **Medigap** insurance, but this still only covers 5 months of Medicare cover. After that everyone is on their financial own.

Over 28 million patients rely on Medicare each year (of whom over 800,000 pay over $2,000 for Medicare during treatment). Life-savings are threatened by any catastrophic illness, or just the need to be in a nursing-home, which costs about $22,000 per person each year (of which only about 2% has been covered by private insurance).

Warning: extras to the above include:

- outpatient drugs
- extra physicians' charges
- eye glasses
- dental costs

It is not unheard of for surviving partners to be left with $10,000 worth of debt upon the death of the sick loved one. This is paid off like a mortgage (say $100 per month, with, if lucky, the balance due at the death of the surviving partner from whatever is left in the estate).

TAXATION

A necessary summary of a necessary evil:

Is there a US version of PAYE?
Yes, but it is calculated in a way quite different from that used in the UK. The system goes something like this:

- *You* estimate what your allowances will be for the coming year.
- A proportion of your salary is excluded from tax on this basis and the rest is taxed at a variable rate plus a flat fee according to income.
- At the end of each tax year you fill in the tax form with the actual (not estimated) allowances. Tax actually due is compared with tax actually paid, and either you pay them or they pay you.

Any good news?
At least the tax year is the calendar year, though the infamous 1040 tax form doesn't have to be submitted until April, to give time for information to be collated.

If this sounds complicated in outline, in practice it's often worse, as the allowances actually allowable are open to dispute.

Any useful short cuts?
- There is a short form for those lucky people with no complications (for instance, no deductions for things like mortgage interest).
- Most people find it pays to use the long form, which means getting professional help. You'll see tax accountants as often as car exhaust

and tyre companies on the edge of shopping malls. The major chain (H & R Block) is as well known as any fast-food firm.

Will it get any simpler?
Reagan's popularity with ordinary voters was partly based upon his promise to simplify government, which for most people means easing not just their tax burden but the burden of doing their taxes. Reagan also promised to do something about national debt. He did — he enlarged it as never before.

Needless to say tax reform has not materialised, though there is a new W-4 form designed to help calculate withholding levels. Paradoxically the new form is 4 pages long, twice the size of what it replaced!

What can I as a foreigner do to simplify my tax?
Pay UK tax if at all possible, and so escape US tax liability (under the treaty principle of being taxed only once on any year's income).

What are the US tax authorities like?
The criminal justice system never got to nail Al Capone. The tax people did, though, and sent him away for a long time for not paying tax on his illegal income. It makes you think. No wonder Americans are often heard saying only two things are certain in life: death and taxes (though not necessarily in that order!).

The IRS can **audit** taxpayers. Audit is a word that conjures up fear and loathing across the USA. The IRS can ask for all written evidence to support your claim for tax allowances for the previous 7 years.

Most taxpayers' returns are not scrutinised — the volume of returns wouldn't allow it. *But* the IRS do undertake *random* examinations, and if anything untoward turns up then an audit may result. Many Americans liken this to shooting hostages, but mostly tax returns are so honestly completed only people pulling a fast one will suffer from an audit.

Does the IRS deal with all income taxes?
The IRS is the *Federal* tax gatherer. Each State is entitles to tax as it sees fit. Most, but not all, do. This means that you have to fill out State *as well as* Federal tax forms, though the State forms are usually simpler, shorter and information from the Federal form can often be reused (and may be cross-checked if there's a feeling you are trying to defraud the system).

Any other taxes?
For the first three years working in the USA you can continue to pay UK National Insurance Contributions. After that you are liable under

the Federal Insurance Contributions Act to contribute to the old-age pension fund and to Medicare (generally for those over 65, or disabled veterans). In the mid 1980s you can reckon on about eight per cent of salary for these deductions. You must have paid for 40 quarters to be eligible. Many payments from these funds can be made available anywhere, and some people retire back to Ireland or to Poland to get the most from their pensions.

Individual States may have their own social welfare taxes, such as a disability insurance scheme taking off another 2% or 3% from salary.

And of course while your overall tax burden may well be lower than in the UK, even when you've added Federal and State payments, you'll still have to pay for your private health and pension plans. The total outgoings from your salary may end up being very familiar to those from Britain (though less than from such countries as Sweden or the Irish Republic). The good news of course is that with an initially higher income you hope to be ahead at the end of the day.

In short: if at all possible avoid being liable for US taxes by continuing to pay UK taxes. Though UK taxes are somewhat higher it's worth the extra to avoid entanglements with the US Internal Revenue Service, whose penalties are greater if you fall foul.

Taxation at a glance

This graph showing relative rates for seven countries provides interesting comparisons. Figures include all compulsory payments to federal, state and local governments for 1983.

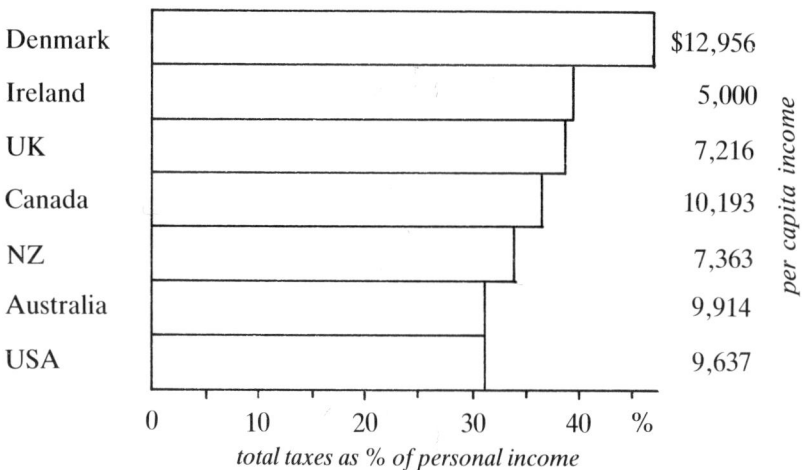

Country	Total taxes as % of personal income	per capita income
Denmark	(bar to ~48%)	$12,956
Ireland	(bar to ~40%)	5,000
UK	(bar to ~38%)	7,216
Canada	(bar to ~35%)	10,193
NZ	(bar to ~33%)	7,363
Australia	(bar to ~31%)	9,914
USA	(bar to ~31%)	9,637

total taxes as % of personal income

Sources: *World Alamanac*, 1984
OECD Revenue Statistics, 1983

These figures should be interpreted with some caution. Australia and the USA may have lower rates than either Britain or Denmark, but Danes are materially the most well off, so beware assuming that tax rates are critical. If you are sick the USA may well help you become bankrupt the fastest.

Where can I read more on this?
Andrew Burgess, *The Expatriate's Guide,* is available for £2.50 including postage and packing from Neville Russell Accountants, 246 Bishopgate, London ED2M 4PB. This well thought out guide outlines the tax consequences of living in the USA. It's written by an ex-Inland Revenue accountant. It may enable you to decide whether or not your financial position needs professional advice.

Nigel A Eastway and David Young's *Expatriate Tax and Investment Guide,* published by Longman in London 1985, is useful, even at £12.50.

There are also magazines for expatriates which may be of interest:

- *Resident Abroad,* 102-108 Clerkenwell Road, London WC1B 3PP
- *The Expatriate,* 25 Brighton Road, South Croydon CR2 6EA
- *EXPATXTRA,* PO Box 300, Jersey, Channel Islands (£25 plus name and address for subscription)

10
The Children and Their Education

...It is often the children who truly lead their elders to America, the sons who take their fathers to their first baseball game or shepherd them to their first rock concert or give them a real sense that they have a stake in America's future.

Henry Grunwald, editor-in-chief, *Time Magazine*
(born in Austria, arrived in the USA aged 17)

Many if not all people emigrate for their children. Safe within their family children are amazingly resilient. They'll pick up the language in weeks not years. They'll play with any child who'll play with them. They'll accept wherever they are as normal. They seem to possess a secret weapon unavailable to their parents.

Parents may be as ambivalent towards the USA as Americans are about them. Parents may keep one eye open towards the old country, following its progress, watching for it on television and in the papers. Their children, however, will not. They live in and for the present, which is now the USA. Where parents need gumption, courage and ambition plus the will to make it their children will have all that and more besides, with no homesickness, no sense of alienation from things American and no feelings of exile. So great may be this feeling of moving forward that parents too may get left behind, seen as old-worldly, accent-ridden, out of touch. The 1985 national spelling contest was won by a 13 year old Tamil student!

Placing a child in the US educational system will be one of the major implications of moving to the USA with a family. Even if you can afford and want to place your children in the private sector there will be remarkable contrasts both with what you remember from your own days at school and from what is going on in Britain today. You may find surprisingly little difference if you are moving from a stable middle class school to one in an equivalent part of the US, but if you are moving a child from a small rural British primary to a large suburban American school the culture shock experienced (not least by yourself) may be immense, just over this aspect of the move. Prepare your child, and thus yourself for the move.

- Talk it through with your child.
- Get to talk with the teacher responsible for your child's pastoral care (who may or may not actually teach them).
- Make sure the school knows the background, educational and otherwise, that your child has experienced to date.
- Take as active an interest in things like the Parent-Teachers' Association (PTA) as you can to keep track of what's going on in the school. This may be particularly necessary if you are not a churchgoer (where many parents will meet, discuss their children and generally keep in touch).
- Don't expect your child's schooling to be like yours was. It wouldn't have been even if you were still back in the UK!
- Don't despair: your child could still return to the UK for third level education if necessary (though this would place a different and perhaps even more unanticipated pressure upon the family, and not necessarily a financial one at that).

THE US EDUCATION SYSTEM

The USA actually has two parallel education systems: one private and one public. In the public sector, which involves about 90% of all pupils and students, control has traditionally been vested in state and local authorities under the general supervision of State Boards of Education, usually appointed by the Governor, though sometimes elected. Each State is divided into school districts, over 16,000 throughout the whole USA, each administered by school boards either elected or appointed locally.

Education is therefore far more locally controlled than it even used to be in Britain. This means that by and large rich areas run well funded schools, poor districts poorly funded schools. However, a widespread concern for civil rights and the belief in the need for a high minimum level of general education had led to the provision of federal funds for the improvement of educational facilities, though not always in the most needy of areas.

Education is by far the greatest item of expenditure for State and local governments, averaging about a third of total spending, being generally lowest in those States where average earnings are depressed. Though southern States have, with some reluctance, come to regard the provision of high quality public schooling for all children regardless of race as an urgent social necessity their generally lower incomes mean that they cannot always afford to improve their educational system.

In rural America, particularly in the West, the level of expenditure is partly dictated by the scattered nature of settlement, making educational costs quite high. Cultural characteristics are also quite important. Minnesota's liberal German and Scandinavian traditions have included considerable support for the adequate funding of education. In the Dakotas, by contrast, a decrease in general levels of prosperity has been reflected in a serious decline in proportionate support for education.

After the Civil War, southern whites were unable to accept the social, economic and political implications of the freeing of the slaves. They were supported by the US Supreme Court which declared that segregation was permissible, provided that facilities for black people were equal to those for whites. In 1954, though, the Supreme Court reversed this 'separate but equal' doctrine, declaring that separation was itself a form of inequality. Federal action followed to integrate the education systems. After the 1964 Civil Rights Act Congress cut off funds to any school district that failed to provide fully integrated education.

Between 1966 and 1972 the once racially segregated public school system of the South was turned around, most dramatically in those States initially most segregated. In the northern States the problem has been focused within the huge cities where segregation, though it surely existed, had not been backed by the force of law.

However, concern with the changing official position has obscured two very important trends: within much of the South white children are now sent to privately funded and segregated schools, often called 'academies', leaving the officially desegregated public schools to the black children, thus defeating the object of Federal policies; and across the North the movement of much of the white population to the suburbs has left officially unsegregated but often totally black schools in the inner cities of huge conurbations. Here the only way to achieve integration has been to bus children from one school district to another, a policy much at odds with the established tradition of neighbourhood schools.

Though the practice of 'bussing' black children away from their local schools to preserve segregation had been long established the introduction of bussing to *integrate* schools came as a rude awakening to many white parents, particularly in those areas that thought the new standards applied only to the South. Widespread resistance followed, and still smoulders. Black students trying to enter once all-white schools have been subjected to verbal abuse and even to physical violence, with law and order only being restored with the arrival of the National Guard.

This kind of lawlessness should not, however, be permitted to over-shadow the amount of social change that has come about, especially in the South. The segregation of so many black children in poor, inner city schools remains, however, a much more intractable issue for American society.

A BEGINNER'S GUIDE TO US SCHOOLS

As if the practical issues of getting a child into school aren't enough, going to school in the USA may turn out to be quite different from the equivalent experience in Britain. The history, geography and literature taught may well change quite dramatically. Religious instruction and prayers are actually forbidden in the public, tax-supported, system. Other ceremonies like the pledge of allegiance, will incorporate your child from day one, and there's little that you can or should do about it.

The groupings of years together in the same school varies from district to district as in Britain (as anyone who has moved into or out of a middle-school district will realise), but the following outline would be widely recognised (a couple of variants are compared to one English norm in the diagram that follows).

Grammar schools (grades 1 to 4) are for those aged 6 to 10, and usually resemble their British primary equivalent (though without the uniforms so beloved of middle-class schools in the UK).

The real contrast will come in both **Junior High** (grades 5 through 9, ages 10 to 13) and **Senior High** (grades 9 through 12, ages 14 to 18) where an amazing lack of discipline and petty rules so prevalent in Britain will be both exciting and frightening, especially for the British pupil making the transition halfway through the system. Younger children will take it more in their stride. For older pupils the lack of discipline will resemble that of going to college, with all its opportunities for individual discovery and the pitfalls of having to work it all out for themselves.

HOW THE US EDUCATION SYSTEM WORKS

Children start school at age 6, and pass through 12 grades, finally 'graduating' at age 18. After that there are community colleges (usually a further two years) or universities (four years). All institutions of learning at whatever level are commonly called 'school'. And *public* schools are just that, schools run for the general public from the public purse.

US school years

Two US variants			A British variant
kindergarten		kindergarten	infants
1 2 3 4 5 6	grade/elementary school	grammar school _ _ _ _ _ _ _ _ _	_ _ _ _ _ primary juniors
7 8	junior high	junior high high	1st 2nd 3rd
9 10 11 12	high school	freshman sophomore junior senior	4th 5th lower sixth upper sixth
1 2 3 4	4 year college	freshman sophomore junior senior	first second final postgraduate

Academic grades

These appear straightforward:

A – very good	worth 4 points	
B – good	3	
C – average	2	
D – poor	1	
F – fail	0	

Grades such as these are given for every essay (paper), exam and course taken, and the grades points average (GPA) calculated (hence 'he's a genius, got a straight four-oh in his senior year'). All grades are internal, and are in comparison to the appropriate peer group. They cannot be compared to GCSE exam results at all. Most grades are from continuous assessment, including marked exercises and short tests rather than lengthy final examinations.

Graduation from high school may be all that's technically required for a place (self-financed though) at the local state-funded college. For entrance to a private college further assessments will probably be required, plus recommendations from teachers.

A few choice words on maths standards

A January 1987 US National Research Council symposium noticed that three new studies showed US school students ranking low among the twenty or so nations considered in mathematical skills (even though US-based standardised scores have actually risen since 1980). This is especially so in geometry and calculus. Only 20% of college-bound US students have ever taken any calculus, deemed essential in applying for any maths degree course elsewhere.

Why such a poor US showing?

- Most Americans see maths ability as innate rather than learned, so if it seems difficult it is because the student is pushing against a locked and bolted door and no amount of teaching or time will ever change anything, so it's best to shift attention to something else.
- US schools generally stress broader, more 'creative' skills such as reading and writing rather than the maths skills emphasised in other countries.
- The use of 'tracking' (assigning students to ability levels) tends to reinforce both good and bad evaluation, with the poorer student giving up completely.
- 'Spiralling' in the curriculum has failed to provide an adequate system for developing advanced skills. Spiralling involves an initially light introduction to maths, returning later to the same concepts at supposedly increasingly sophisticated levels. But in practice it has students revisiting the same material again and again, covering much the same ground at about the same level, with boredom setting in all around.
- All-purpose teachers, especially at early grades, are used rather than well-trained maths specialists.
- Geometry and algebra are only introduced after students are more than half way through the 12 year programme; elsewhere the ideas have already been introduced, if only very generally, much earlier.

Who runs the schools?

The decentralised administrative system of the USA deeply influences the public schools. They are run not by counties but by specially constituted **school boards,** who have to raise money locally from taxes.

By and large school boards in well-to-do areas have the money to maintain the schools, pay attractive salaries, and suitably equip the libraries and laboratories. In poor areas the converse happens. Government grants are available in target areas (say if a school is next to an airforce base which influences the student intake and may overburden the local tax base).

Federal monies may be available for remedial programmes, but by and large schools reflect the local tax base. As this shifts so does the quality of the schools.

General points worth considering

- **Size**

  Often much bigger than (traditionally at least) in Britain. A graduating year may reach 1,000. Hence the number of yellow school buses out on the roads!

- **Assembly**

  In the British 1944 Education Act sense assemblies don't exist in the USA. The US Constitution requires the separation of State and religion, so religious observances far from being required are forbidden (and would be deemed divisive).

- **Sport**

  Low key, which may be a surprise given the high profile nature of much school competitive sport. Most effort goes into the school teams, so 'jocks' get most of the attention. Physical education classes may be the nearest to playing sport most students ever get, which may explain the popularity of 'Little League' baseball out of school hours, and the success of school soccer (and it's less expensive and less dangerous than American football!).

- **Uniform**

  In all but a very few select private schools (pretending to be British prep schools or else pseudo-military academies) uniform is unheard of (like most of continental Europe).

PRIVATE EDUCATION

Across the whole range, from kindergarten to graduate school, private education parallels the public system. This is based upon two things:

Money

The first is the desire to *buy* a better education for the children. As in Britain a bought education is not necessarily better than what is publicly available, but so long as people are looking for conspicuous consumption *and* an edge over other people the private schools will continue to have a social cachet if nothing else.

The east coast tends to have two main variations:

- the military, usually but not always, southern-based school where military style uniforms, discipline and hygiene are imposed upon a chosen few

- 'prep' schools, preparing students for college, usually prestigious 'Ivy League' ones (hence the term 'preppy' for an American Sloane Ranger).

Both types are rare out west, being seen as too European, and thus more suited to a supposedly more decadent east.

Religious principles

Since religion is excluded from the public schools by the US Constitution, private schools based on religious principles have developed. 'Parochial' schools range from the sort of convent schools or Roman Catholic schools that you'd find in the UK, through to fundamentalist academies which might be a little too vigorous for British tastes, even for those of a religious persuasion themselves.

Unfortunately too many new parochial schools, especially in the South, are merely attempts to create all-white schools given that the public schools have been racially integrated.

Perhaps the same applies to secular schools – those run on experimental lines for usually well-to-do liberal progressive parents.

THE IMPLICATIONS OF EDUCATION IN THE USA

In the whole range of everyday activities things won't be quite the way they were back home. Moreover, your children will not be yours for very much longer. This would be equally true if you had stayed where you were. But taking them to the USA and immersing them in American society means that it may well seem all that much more dramatic. The values, habits and expectations they pick up will be from people who do not necessarily share the same cultural background, even more so than had you stayed at home. Rather the children will come back to you ever more American as each day passes. And while there will be good things about this, aspects of which you will approve, there will also be things of which you may strongly disapprove.

Growing up in the USA

It has long been taken for granted that middle-class children get some kind of job as early as possible, if only around their own yard (that is, the garden). Children are after all in training for an adulthood of getting and spending.

Babysitting is often a daughter's first experience with the great world of work. If you have young children you'll find that local junior high school students will expect to babysit for you (as they will expect you to buy Girl Scout cookies from them in due season). The babysitter may well bring her young sibling along with her (so doing two jobs at once). These even younger would-be earners may well return in due course ready and eager to haggle with you over garden chores you might have been expecting that you or your children would do as a matter of course. Watering the lawn and flower beds is a great favourite for those too young to babysit but not too young to spend. Television assures an intimate knowledge of every possible product aimed at children whether cloths, foods, drinks or toys. If you live in a condominium apartment complex where the children may not be able to offer gardening services they will still find ways of earning money, if only watering the plants and feeding the cat when you are away.

By high school mere babysitting will have been supplemented by working in the local ice-cream parlour, fast-food outlets, dog-walking, bagging-up or even cashiering in local stores. It is all good preparation for 'working your way through college', and through life come to that.

US children seem to grow up quickly. In this they are generally encouraged by families, neighbours, and friends. if you believe that everything should be in its due season you may be seen as sheltering your children from the harsh fact of life. Children are introduced very early to that most American of claims: 'there is no free lunch'.

How to respond?

- Talk things through with your children. They may actually prefer to get paid for mowing the lawn (like their friends) rather than have a set amount of pocket money come what may. The children have to live with their friends; though no-strings pocket money may sound great it may not be as good as doing what everyone else at that age does.

- Your children will want to be exactly like their US friends, rather than like you. They will say the pledge of allegiance along with everyone else even if you are only in the US for a fixed period. After all, as grown-ups you wouldn't want to be excluded from the 4th July party just because you are foreigners!

What can I read about US education?

There's not a lot available outside the USA. You may be able to order the following couple of critical exposes, both by a (not the) David Owen, *High School,* Viking, New York, 1981 and *None of the Above* (the title echoing the last choice on a multiple-choice test), Houghton Mifflin, New York, 1985. For an extremely jaundiced view of being an American student see Allen Bloom's *The Closing of the American Mind,* Simon & Schuster, New York 1987 (reviewed for a British audience in *The Listener* 25 June 1987, pp.26-27, obtainable via your local public or college library).

GOING TO COLLEGE

Where once upon a time twelve years of schooling was supposed to be enough to give the immigrant and native alike a sufficient leg-up to do well in the US job market, and thus in life, a further four years of college is a minimum prerequisite these days. A further two years of postgraduate work are also highly desirable. This is due to the growing sophistication of the job market and the corollary that twelve years of schooling prepares people for very little these days. Compared to British sixth-formers most American high school seniors are a couple of years behind academically.

Middle class American students display a far greater sense of optimism than their British equivalent. They may seem to talk about 'nukes', nuclear winters and nuclear half-lives, but their unselfconscious optimism seems to surround them with a protective shield. For them Armageddon isn't real. Their good will defeat anyone else's evil. They may be publicly cynical about 'the system', but they will never doubt that this century belongs to the USA. They are on the winning side, the side of democracy.

Such myopic optimism may seem little more than the positive thinking of a prosperous society, but it also comes from the kind of education they receive. Debate as understood in the UK is quite rare for school children. The political system that they learn about in Civics classes, and which they follow through the congressional hearings on television (Watergate to Irangate) is quite a different political system than in Britain.

Congress's role is to act as a check upon the executive. On the floor of the House of Representatives members do not argue, that is debate by a series of arguments laid out to sustain an internally consistent line of thought. Rather members make speeches that will get into the papers, or if they are lucky, get onto the TV news back in their home State. Students themselves don't debate as such but hold arguments that are often little more than rows, people talking past each other.

By the time high school students have moved on to college they often come over as amazingly erudite. Talk to them and you feel you are talking to really educated people, even if you can't quite put your finger upon what it is they have been educated in. But they are amazingly aware, interested, studious even (if there's a test due). They have done courses in subjects that British high-fliers have only heard of: nutrition, family dynamics, even 'world history'. And their more traditional courses seem so well focused upon the 'now' of it all: feminism in George Eliot, Stonehenge as a proto-computer, or Chinese history (since Nixon let them be friends and business-partners with this particular group of 'Reds'). Everything comes to be channelled towards tomorrow's big chance. It's all very professional. No knowledge for knowledge's sake, or even as a hobby (leave that for retirement). All are being educated for the job market whether coming to it from the humanities, the social sciences or the natural sciences.

College entrance tests

High school graduates wanting to go to college have no standardised examination results like 'A' levels to offer the college of their choice. The grades of each school cannot be usefully compared one with another. To cope with this many students take SATs, that is **Scholastic Aptitude Tests,** held by the Educational Testing Service for those who want to go somewhere other than to their local State college. By the mid-1980s over $1\frac{1}{2}$ million students were taking SATs each year. And this despite the repeated criticisms made of such tests.

At worst SATs are accused of testing nothing but a student's ability to take the SATs themselves. At best they are seen as assuming all students share a common white, upper-middle class, suburban point of view. The existence of cramming colleges that teach, for instance, the meaning of the hundred most commonly tested word definitions (for example: enigma and apathy) suggests claims that SATs test only aptitude rather than any particular body of knowledge are shaky. Still, be aware that such tests, warts and all, do exist.

There is an equivalent for those graduating from college, the **Graduate Aptitude Test** (GAT). Some foreign applicants are asked to take such tests (at various UK centres) but most foreign student offices will waive SATs or GATs for well documented foreign applicants.

- A perfect SAT score is 1,600 (800 mathematical 800 verbal skills)
  US norm is 897 (461 and 426)

Evidence from cramming courses suggests that SAT scores can be raised from 100 to 175 (even up to 250 for very exceptional cases), though ETS organisers maintain that cramming can only produce more modest improvements of from 14 to 26 points.

Much more important for someone moving to the USA from Britain is to have all transcripts, certificates and exam results available for the US school or college. Most higher education institutions in Britain can supply results with a note of explanation written for US schools and colleges (originally designed for US students doing their ritual 'junior year abroad' at a British college).

The traditional British put-down of the American high school graduate and the self-satisfied observation that their first two years at college raise Americans to about 'A' level standard should not blind the British arrival to the fact that US graduates, those who complete the four years at college, are at least as competent as their British equivalents, or put another way:

- it's easier to get into college in the USA,
- but just as hard to get out.

In most States publicly funded colleges admit state residents who have graduated from high school. This means that first-year undergraduate classes are *huge* (200-300 per lecture, 30-40 per 'discussion group' where the lecture and this week's chapter and exercises are gone over in more detail). Exams are set so that vast numbers of students (usually a pre-set percentage) will fail.

Those who survive this in-house selection of the first couple of years 'elect a major', that is declare to the college which subject they want to specialise and so graduate in. They then proceed to choose from the college catalogue those courses that when added together constitute a degree programme. Each course is usually self-contained, with tests and exercises most weeks, with a longer term paper (essay) plus a final, written exam at the very end of the course. Each course successfully completed provides credit plus grades, markers on the way to graduation.

At the end of the programme, which is supposed to last four years (but can last as long as the money and stamina remain available for weaker or poorer students), those with the highest grade point averages may graduate *Summa cum Laude* (excellent), *Magna cum Laude* (very good), or on the *Dean's List* (good).

College terms

Terms are generally called **semesters,** of which there are two, Fall and

Spring, each lasting about 14 weeks, with some places having a break about midway. At the time of 'spring break' thousands of students swarm south to the beaches. The papers go wild with talk of 'sex and drugs and rock 'n' roll' in places like Fort Lauderdale, Florida.

Semesters run from late August to Christmas, and January to May. For those who missed or failed a course and wish to catch up shorter, more intensive 8 week courses are offered between two semesters in **summer school**, when staff, often on auto-pilot, teach again at great speed what they've just taught earlier in the year, but for extra money.

Fees

As publicly financed institutions, State universities and community colleges generally waive tuition fees for people from within that State. All others pay 'out of State fees', which can be hefty. This naturally encourages students to stay within their own State.

But remember that most States are the size of countries elsewhere, so many still have to leave home to go to college. Even with free tuition there are still 'nominal' registration fees, health centre fees, sports centre fees, all of which must be paid at the beginning of the semester (and don't forget that parking lot fee too!).

And of course if you want to live on campus in a **dormitory** (hall of residence) you will have to pay a residence fee for accommodation, and these are not grant-aided. Over four years even a 'free' college education can be expensive. How, then, do students manage it?

- Living at home may be necessary just to survive. For parents this means supporting an adult until they are at least 22!
- Part-time work, which can mean anything, just to raise cash for books, clothes, etc, even where parents provide the accommodation. In college towns most menial and service jobs, such as in fast-food outlets, are held by students.
- Work-study, where government or the college provide students with menial work for low pay.
- Loans, repayable upon graduation, whether governmental or commercial.

Financing a college education

Ronald Reagan once starred in *She's Working Her Way Through College* in which a burlesque star tries to better herself by going to college, promoting the US ideal that students should be both willing and able to work their way through college, so becoming free of both parents and the State. The reality today, however, tends to be otherwise. By 1985 less than 4% of the average student's financial package came from work as against just under 45% grants and almost 52% loans. The soaring costs of college and diminishing federal support means that commercial loans are becoming ever more necessary.

Work-study programmes provide help with fees in exchange for working in the college itself. In 1985 some 870,000 students nationwide worked on federally funded work-study programmes, but the maximum is 12 hours per week during term time, and the pay is the legal $3.50 hourly minimum, and as it involves mostly washing floors, dishes and serving food hardly amounts to vocational training.

Some universities hire their own students to do the menial work. Each year, for instance, the University of Minnesota hires 17,000 of its students up to 29 hours each, with a yearly pay bill of about $70 million. But financial pressures bearing down upon college budgets at least as hard as upon individual students there's always the temptation to cut down upon financial support except for those in dire need or for those sporting or high-flying students likely to bring credit to the college. Everywhere the need for student loans seems on the rise.

Loans are becoming even more necessary. The best are at fixed low-interest rates not repayable until after graduation. In the past these have tended to be governmental, or underwritten by government, but so many people disappeared after graduation and never paid up that the authorities have tried to end these altogether. **Commercial loans,** preferably based upon parental collateral, are ever more important. In 1986 students and their parents borrowed some $10,000 million. This all places graduating students under great pressure to get good well-paid jobs as soon as possible, with many socially necessary but not so well-paid jobs (including college teaching!) being far less attractive than well-paid legal and commercial jobs. This skewing of the job market is getting quite serious in places.

Private colleges
Many world famous US universities are private foundations, but be sure to distinguish between those of social status and those with high academic standing. The most prestigious universities in popular standing are the **Ivy League** (Brown, Cornell, Dartmouth, University of Pennsylvania, Princeton, Columbia, Yale and Harvard), so called because of their 'ancient', ivy-on-the-wall, standing. Together with once all-girls colleges such as Vassar and Smith these form a self-sustaining first division, though for many this rests upon high social standing as much as upon world renown.

The Massachusetts Institute of Technology outside Boston is at least as world renowned as Harvard, but like other institutions such as Stanford on the West Coast, has a 'boffin' image. There are also a large number of often quite small, sometimes experimental, colleges right across the country.

All tend to be expensive. 'If you need to ask the cost you can't afford them' is a pretty good rule of thumb.

How to choose a college?

If you decide to send your offspring to a US college, rather than fly them back to the UK for a British education (which may be cheaper and possibly better if you choose well) it is very much a question of detective work, asking other parents of college-age children, reading prospectuses **(catalogues)** and if possible visiting the campus and appropriate departments. Do you really want your 18 year old to go to a State university, living at home, commuting every day (along with maybe 10,000 other drivers) onto a campus of 35,000 students, where classes will be in vast lecture rooms seating 300 at one go, being taught in classes of about 35 students a time by overworked and underpaid postgraduates **(teaching assistants)**? The same university might be just the place for postgraduate work after graduation elsewhere. Graduate classes will be of about a dozen, with sustained personal contact with senior staff over several years, with access to facilities only a vast state university library and laboratories could offer.

'It's all Greek to me'

The film *Animal House* may have introduced the notion of **fraternities** (for men) and **sororities** (for women) to a British audience. Fear not, such excesses as portrayed there are as likely as the school rebellion in the British film *If*. Nevertheless, it's useful to know something about these institutions, if only to know what to avoid:

- **Greeks** – members of societies so called because of their use of three Greek letters, such as Delta Beta Phi.
- **Frat house** – houses owned by *Greek* societies, usually on the edge of campus, providing room and board for members.
- **Rushes** – recruitment of new members, which can involve recruits passing through initiation rites (often masonic by way of Monty Python).
- **Honor societies** – undergraduate societies that recruit students with excellent grade averages for social and academic functions (rather like subject-based societies at British universities, but nationally based, as with the Geographers' Gamma Theta Upsilon).
- **Greek week** – a week for 'fun' activities run by fraternities and sororities (resembling a rag week in the exuberance, high-jinks and potential for mayhem).

11
Opportunities for Young People and Teachers

SHORT TERM OPPORTUNITIES

There are many easily found packages for those with money to spend: visit any good travel agent. For those who need to work their way across there are basically two routes:

- Work over here and spend over there – see David Leppard, *The Directory of Summer Jobs in Britain,* available from Vacation Work Publications, 9 Park End Street, Oxford (annually about £7).
- Work overseas and spend time and money in the USA – see David Leppard, *The Directory of Jobs and Careers Abroad,* also available from Vacation Work Publications (about £7). This deals with a wide range of countries (not just in North America).

The most usual and still highly popular jobs in the USA are:

- summer camps
- au pairing

It is quite possible to arrange jobs unaided by specialists, but it's likely to be more convoluted, time-consuming and risky. You can find information on US summer jobs in:

- US newspapers
- US magazines
- via US contracts
- by writing to US branches of groups you may deal with over here, such as the YMCA, YHA, Scouts.

If you do get a job this way you'll have to pay your own ticket (which might be a financial blow) but you'll get to keep your final pay: it'll be yours, which wouldn't be the case if you've used a broker (like Camp America). You may be able to negotiate a better deal than you'll get if you go through an agency. But you may be ripped off, exploited, sacked or worse. You take the risk (and it may well pay off).

If you've little room for manoeuvre you may have to go through an intermediary. At least that way your papers will certainly be in order. The leading intermediary is **Camp America,** with origins 18 years ago in **BUNAC** — the British Universities North American Club.

SUMMER CAMPS

If you are a student, a teacher or a nurse and are over 18 then Camp America may be able to provide you with a 9 week job in the USA teaching sports, arts and crafts, or camping and other outdoor skills in US summer camps.

Benefits include the right paperwork for US Immigration, free return flight, board and lodgings, pocket money, and free time for your own travel plans at the end of the job before flying back home. Contact Address.

- **Camp America,** 37 Queens Gate, LONDON SW7 5HR ((01) 581 2378)

In 1986 Camp America placed over 4,000 applicants in summer camps in the USA, finding places for 85% of British applicants. Though round-trip fare is included you will be required to provide a £25 deposit by February, and a further £60 when placed. If you are one of the unlucky ones for whom no place is found the initial £25 is refunded.

When?
The US summer is somewhat earlier than that in the UK so you'd need to plan accordingly. Summer starts when school gets out, which can be as early as the third week in May. Summer camps are well underway by the end of June, so you should be able to leave Britain no later than the 28th June, preferably a little earlier. As summer formally ends with the first Monday of September (Labor Day) summer camps end by about 26th August. Then you'll have time to travel until you're due back in Britain.

How can I find out what it's like?
- Ask around at college.
- Write to **Camp America**
- Attend their **Recruitment Weekend** held in London towards the end of February. Here you'll be able to meet and talk with directors of US camps interested in hiring British counsellors.

What do I need to apply?
- A character reference.
- A curriculum vitae (CV) stating your skills, qualifications, and what you've done that make you suitable for the job.
- Three good passport sized photographs.
- Any sporting, teaching or professional certificates you can produce to support your application.

AU PAIRING

British au pairs have traditionally been in great demand in the USA, even where cheaper local or Mexican help is readily available. This has something to do with the snob value of having someone from Europe, someone a little bit exotic but who speaks English. Any British accent is deemed high class and so desirable (at least among the class of people who want and can afford to hire au pairs).

How do I find out what it's all about?
- Write to **Camp America**, Family Companion/Au Pair Department, 37 Queens Gate, LONDON SW7 5HR ((01) 581 2378)
- Attend the **Camp America London Recruitment Weekend** held towards the end of February each year for those who can spend the *entire* year in the USA.

Can I do it without such help?
- The US authorities are tightening up their responses to US residents hiring people who lack the necessary papers to work in the USA. In practical terms it's unlikely that people staying on after a holiday would ever be found out, but you would have to be prepared to live in something of a limbo, and if you do get caught you may find that deportation will mean you won't be allowed to re-enter the USA again.
- Camp America provide a fully legal service based upon 18 years of dealing with the appropriate US paperwork.
- They also have the contacts built up over the years.
- You might be able to find a suitable employer from this distance, but even if you made contact you are taking a far greater risk than when going through an agency that in effect acts as a vetting process, for both employer and employee.
- If you organise everything yourself and things don't work out who can you turn to? Camp America has US contacts.
- If you do everything for yourself and it works well you will of course stand to make more money: your employer won't have any agency fees to pay.

What do I need to apply?
- Three good passport sized photographs
- A character reference.
- A curriculum vitae (CV) setting out what you've done, what skills and qualification you have.
- Any sporting, teaching or professional certificates you have to support your application.

WORKING IN WASHINGTON DC

Thousands of young Americans regularly work in the offices of the US Congress. An estimated 19,000 more swell the staff of political think-tanks, lobby groups, media and business institutions, or work in the State Department, the White House, or elsewhere in the administration. These high-fliers enjoy positions of prestige that will place them on the road to further privilege. The bad news is that these **interns,** as they are known, are paid little if anything. The pay-off comes in the experience, the connections and their enhanced CV (or resumé as they'd say). It is an investment in their future whether or not they envisage a future in politics or public administration.

Increasingly students are placed in **programmed internships** by their own college working through college representatives permanently stationed in the capital. Students get course credit towards their degrees in exchange for writing a report on their experience. The best programmes are carefully scrutinised by academics knowledgeable in the ways of Washington politics to ensure that interns are more than office dogsbodies. With the local University of Maryland alone providing 600 interns per year there is demand and supply far exceeding anything found in British local government or even Westminster. Congress alone employs about 5,000 interns per year, who gain first-hand experience of the legislative process, lobbying and wheeler-dealer.

Competition for internships in fierce. There are over 200 applications form each place in a senator's office. Preference is given to people from the home constituency, particularly those already known to the senator or representative in the election campaign that brought them into office.

Interns answer the telephone, answer constituents' mail (using word processors, form letters and machines that 'sign' outgoing constituency mail), may attend meetings of Congress to prepare memos and report on matters of concern, and may get to draft position papers based upon library research.

Non-governmental options go through a clearing house: **The Washington Centre**, 1101 14th Street NW, Washington DC 20005 ((202) 289 8680), which ensures a quality placement, laying on courses and seminars for over 600 colleges. It ensures that no more than 20% of the intern's time is spent on mundane clerical work. In 1986 a ten-week internship cost about £600 (plus £600 housing and meals). The think-tanks are privately sponsored research and policy monitoring institutions such as the conservative **Heritage Foundation**, 214 Massachusets Avenue NE, Washington DC 20002 ((202) 546 4400) which has 17 summer programme places each paying about £120 a week, or the (liberal) **Institute for Policy Studies,** 1901 'Q' Street NW, Washington DC 20009 ((202)234 9382). Another avenue would be the *Student Guide to Mass Media Internships* (1984) published by the School of Journalism, Boulder, Colorado, which lists 2,000 different internships in the USA (newspapers, magazines, television, radio, and publishing). Hands-on experience prior to a formal job-search would be good for the old CV.

Few British students participate, but doing an exchange year in the USA may make it possible via your US college's own programme. Some British students with family connections in the USA have worked 'on the Hill' as it's called, but without remuneration. British students in the USA as 'resident aliens' may be able to work in the office of their local representative as part of a US- based degree course. If still interested in working on Capitol Hill contact:

- Bernie Muller, Intern Program Director, US Congress, WASHINGTON DC 20515

APPLYING FOR SUMMER JOBS

Before an employer can employ a foreign student s/he must be willing to obtain, fill out and submit all the necessary US government forms. Remember the basic rule is that foreigners cannot take jobs in the USA. The paperwork makes a case for exceptions to this general rule. It means time and effort for the employer, for little if any immediate gain if people already in the USA could be readily hired. So be prepared to ask an employer if such paperwork can be arranged, and arranged soon enough for a visa to be issued.

Joining such organisations as the British Universities North America Club (BUNAC) or Camp America can help with the paper work as:

- they are familiar with what's needed
- they deal with US contacts also familiar with the problems
- a US sponsor is required by the US authorities – that can't be done alone.

Even if you arrange something on your own it may help to obtain the kind of advice available only through groups such as BUNAC or Camp America.

It helps to understand what is involved. As a general rule there are only three types of visas suitable for foreign students who will be returning home after their summer employment:

H-2 'Temporary Worker'

This requires a US employer to obtain a 'labor certification' from the local state employment service. The US Department of Labor requires evidence that:

- a real job exists
- reasonable effort has already been made to fill the job from within the USA
- no qualified US resident has applied.

> *Example:* Camp Manhattan takes a lot of Canadian children for whom a French-speaking canoe instructor is always hired. This year though, despite advertising in college newspapers since October, no suitable applicant has applied. Then a British canoeist who's just spent a year at a French college applies. The camp wants to hire him, and is prepared to do the paperwork. Certification would be granted as a legitimate case has been made.

H-3 'Industrial Trainee'

Here no labor certification is required, but any application must include:

- a detailed training plan
- a training/on-the-job breakdown
- an explanation as to why this training cannot be obtained in the applicant's home country.

> *Example:* Camp Manhattan prides itself in the quality of its management, and especially its own camp counsellor in-house training programme. A British student who's worked in a British day camp writes asking if she can join their programme for residential experience. The Camp organisers could submit the necessary details for an H-3 visa, *but* it might well be rejected if the Immigration and Naturalization Service believe it's just a fiddle to get someone's British girlfriend into the USA for a paid summer job.

J-1 'Exchange Visitor'

These visas are *only* available for applicants participating in educational programmes specifically approved by the US Information Agency. Approved **Exchange Visitor Programs** are granted only to US sponsoring organisations such as US government agencies, colleges, hospitals and private educational organisations.

The **Council on International Educational Exchange** (205 East 42nd Street, New York, NY 10017) in cooperation with BUNAC has a J-1 authorisation for a summer 'work-travel' programme. This programme permits students to work on any job they can find (though *not* to undertake practical training or summer camp positions). No extensions or visa changes are permitted.

J-1 summer camp placements are authorised for the **International Camp Counsellor Program** of the YMCA (356 West 34th Street, 3rd floor, New York, NY 10001), with an 8 week limit, and must involve counselling or skills instruction rather than kitchen or office jobs.

Paid practical training is organised via a number of sponsors have J-1 programmes such as the **International Association of Students in Economics and Business Management** (AIESEC), 14 West 23rd Street, New York, NY 10010, and the **International Association for Exchange of Students for Technical Experience** (IAESTE) Trainee Programme, c/o Association for International Practical Training, 10480 Little Patuxet, Suite 320, Columbia, Maryland 21044. The maximum length of practical training time for any one person is 18 months.

What happens now?
- H-2 and H-3 visa applications, if successful, will lead to the US Embassy being so informed, where the visa will be issued to the student presenting a valid passport.
- J-1 applications, if successful, lead to sponsoring organisations issuing a 'Certificate of Eligibility' (IAP-66) to be taken, plus passport, to the US Embassy.
- Upon entering the USA the immigration inspector will issue form 1-94 upon which the visa type and maximum stay date are recorded.

How difficult is it?
The process takes time. Securing a visa can take up to six months, so start early, at the beginning of the academic year. When contacting prospective employers let them know which visa you are seeking, which sponsoring organisation (if any), and which forms they would need to submit, if any.

A word of warning
The summer officially ends on Labor Day (first Monday in September). Colleges and schools start back in the last week of August. If you don't intend to return to Britain before the end of September (say for a British university term) you may have difficulty persuading US officials that

intending to return that late in the year isn't incompatible with being a student. You'll need to explain when term starts (and that your term didn't end until early July rather than late May).

FURTHER OPPORTUNITIES FOR STUDENTS

Many **grants** and **scholarships** exist for travel and study in the USA. Most British universities and colleges have careers offices which can usually make available details of such awards. Many awards are open to people from particular areas or doing research into particular topics. One Welsh student at Keele University who had hated being made to take Welsh 'O' level found a US scholarship was available to people from her parents' home town who could apply in Welsh. Her 'O' level suddenly became a much treasured skill. And so off she went to South Dakota!

Historians might apply to the **American Antiquarian Society,** 185 Salisbury Street, Worcester, Massachusetts 01609, concerning research stipends of up to $1,800 for a one to three month research visit associated with writing a dissertation on a pre-1876 subject. For UK postgraduate students such a fellowship could be invaluable. Holders of ESRC awards for doctoral research are automatically told about their eligibility concerning travel and living allowances for any research necessary in the USA.

LONG-TERM OPPORTUNITIES

Colleges vary in quality of education provided, prestige, location (which might crucially influence your access to research materials) and costs. Most British students fending for themselves will be postgraduates. Undergraduates by and large go to US colleges on paid-for exchanges, regulated, approved and monitored by their own UK college, or are already in the US as immigrants. Postgraduates are usually there under their own steam, so the cost of living becomes crucial.

Most Britsh postgraduate students in the USA are financing themselves by part-time teaching at the college where they are registered. Payment is by a **graduate stipend,** which usually comes every two weeks in the form of a cheque that must then be deposited before cash is forthcoming. Being a vast place the US has a cost of living that varies enormously from town to town and you'll need to take this into account when evaluating possible places to study.

As can be seen in the table below the effective value of a postgraduate teaching assistant stipend can vary enormously, with a California stipend almost twice that of somewhere in the Midwest. But, and it's a big

Graduate Student Stipends, Adjusted for Cost
of Living in Selected Urban Areas

Geography Department	1985/86 Stipend*	1986/87 Adjusted stipend**
University of California (Los Angeles)	$8,653	$7,597
University of Maryland (College Park)	6,935	5,561
University of Washington (Seattle)	6,396	5,972
Ohio State University (Columbus)	6,219	6,164
University of Colorado (Boulder)	6,194	5,714
State University of New York (Buffalo)	5,854	6,073
Pennsylvania State University (State College)	5,560	5,756
University of Illinois (Chicago)	5,296	4,973
University of North Carolina (Chapel Hill)	4,731	4,652
University of Missouri (Columbia)	4,572	5,120
Indiana State University (Terre Haute)	4,282	4,479

*These data were compiled for the US Council for Graduate Schools. The stipend listed is the average state stipend *after* any required tuition fees have been paid.
**The adjustment was made using the fourth-quarter 1985 composite 'intercity cost of living indicator', as compiled by the American Chamber of Commerce Research Association.

but, even income adjusted for cost of living factors still gives only an indication of the true costs and benefits. For some people Los Angeles might be intolerable at any price. For a lone British postgraduate, without friends and family for support, Los Angeles without a car might be far less satisfying than a Midwestern college town with less money, where you could walk to work, save up for a car, and visit the big cities with new college friends as and when chances present themselves. And what is the cost of living anyway? Do you expect to have your own flat immediately upon arrival or would you share? But would you share a room with a fellow student? Would you walk or hitch-hike to work? Are you on your own, or with a wife not herself allowed to work by visa regulations?

If you are single, able-bodied, and prepared to be flexible upon your arrival, getting a graduate stipend should solve not just your visa problems but keep you with a roof over your head. And if that doesn't always work out many graduates have made long-standing — though supposedly temporary — nests in their office on campus — while intending to look for somewhere else of course! For a married student survival is possible, but can be financially very tight and demoralising for the non-working partner. And there's always the risk of being forced into the black economy and so risking your status.

The advice of experience is: **go**, if at all possible. It's worth it for the experience. And with an academic department as your base, a place to live in, people to share with, old cars to borrow or even to buy, things always turn up via the grapevine. Americans are proverbially hospitable, and no more so when they hear of someone at the office sleeping in a bag on the floor or walking to work from an unfurnished apartment.

POSTGRADUATE SCHOLARSHIPS

There are four well-known UK scholarships specifically available for British postgraduate students wishing to study in the USA: **Fulbright, Thouron, Kennedy** and **Harkness.**

Fulbright scholarships
These are available for travel and maintenance for British UK-based postgraduates for 'a year of advanced study research in the United States'. Applications must be submitted by 30th October each year. Details and application forms from:

- Fulbright Commission, 6 Porter Street, LONDON WIM 2HR ((01) 486 7697)

Thouron awards

The Thouron-University of Pennsylvania Fund for British-American Student Exchange offers six awards covering maintenance and fees for study at the University of Pennsylvania (in Philadelphia). In 1987 these amounted to $825 per month maintenance plus $1,800 fees for the duration of the scholar's course. Closing date is the 6th November each year. Details can be obtained from:

- The Registrar, Thouron Awards, The University of Glasgow, GLASGOW G12 8QQ

Kennedy scholarships

These are for postgraduate study at Harvard or the Massachusetts Institute of Technology. Twelve scholarships exist to cover tuition, health care, travel and maintenance, providing an allowance of $9,000 in the first year, $7,940 if renewed. Prospectus and application forms from:

- The Secretary, Kennedy Memorial Trust, 16 Great College Street, LONDON SW1P 3RX

Closing date for applications is the third week in October.

Harkness fellowships

These are for UK educated graduates, professionals, journalists or creative artists under 33 years old on 1st September of the year of application, which must be made by 8th October for interviewing the following February. For full application materials write to:

- The Harkness Fellowships, Harkness House, 38 Upper Brook Street, LONDON W1Y 1PE

enclosing a self-addressed 10″ by 7″ envelope stamped with 31 pence postage. Fellowships are highly competitive, and cover fares, car hire, living and family allowances, tuition and research costs, and health care insurance.

POSTRADUATE DEGREES

In the US the word postgraduate is always shortened to just **graduate.** Large universities usually offer both Master's and Doctoral programmes, though smaller institutions might only offer graduate courses to the Master's level. If you would like to carry straight through at the same institution you need to check up on this very early in the process.

Master of Arts (MA)

MA programmes are designed primarily for students who wish to acquire a further degree but who also wish primarily to make their career within the world beyond education, whether in business or government. Courses generally last one year for full-time students, a minimum of two years for part-timers. Programmes are by taught courses followed by either a thesis or at least two research papers. The programme provides a firm theoretical and methodological foundation for either moving on to the doctoral level, or for a move out into the wider job market, which increasingly requires an MA rather than a BA, as more and more people complete the first degree.

Doctor of Philosophy (PhD)

PhD programmes are more complicated than in Britain, usually requiring considerable high-level taught courses (which might be in statistics, computing, languages or philosophy irrespective of the main field) before progressing to the preparation of a lengthy research dissertation. It is usual for the PhD stage to take at least three years after the two years spent on the master's degree, a total of at least five years, with the writing up often taking a further couple of years. As most people will be in employment in order to pay the bills by this time it can be very difficult to complete, especially if work takes you away from your university to live elsewhere, and if growing career and family demands gradually ease the PhD to one side. Beware: completion must be within a pre-set timetable, and unlike the UK situation cannot be extended almost indefinitely.

How to apply

If you wish to apply for (post-)graduate work in the USA you should first write to the **heads of departments** you might be interested in asking for general details. Technically you should write directly to the Director of Graduate Studies at each institution asking for forms and additional information, but procedures seem to be more relaxed for foreign applicants.

Be prepared to write to a wide range of universities, and don't be bothered by the vast number who never even reply. A dozen letters for two or three replies might not be unusual. Twenty initial enquiries is not unusual. Those that do reply are usually taking your application seriously.

In theory you should be prepared to supply:

- three letters of recommendation
- GRE scores (1,000 minimum)

- college records ('transcripts') of all previous academic work showing a grade point average of at least 3.0 or equivalent
- proof of proficiency in English, usually waived for applicants from English-speaking countries
- proof of sufficient funds to pay all fees and expenses for at least one year

Universities that deal regularly with certain foreign countries' applicants may waive the need to take a GRE exam and may automatically assume you will need to apply for financial aid both to get the visa and of course to stay alive.

For anyone wishing to be considered for financial aid all applications, letters of recommendation, etc, *must* be received by the US institution by 1st February for entry the following August.

There is no readily available guidebook for would-be graduate students seeking to study in US colleges. However, most university and polytechnic career advice centres should be able to discuss opportunities and ways of approaching US institutions, and may well have copies of US catalogues (prospectuses).

OPPORTUNITIES FOR TEACHERS

Teachers wishing to spend time in the USA might like to consider a scholarship specially geared to their needs, or a post-to-post exchange with someone.

Teacher scholarships.
These are organised by the **English Speaking Union** to enable participants to explore their field of study within the USA and to become more broadly acquainted with American life. There are two main sets of scholarships

- **the Walter Hines Page Scholarship** for 8-week term-time visits (October to May) and
- **Chautauqua Institution Scholarships** for a 9-week summer school-based tour.

Other Page scholarships for shorter (4-week) visits are sponsored by teaching unions and associations such as NASWT and NUT. There is fortunately an introductory leaflet which gives details of where to apply. Write to:

- The Director of Education, The English-Speaking Union, Dartmouth House, 37 Charles Street, LONDON W1X 8AB

Applications usually have to be submitted by the end of November for the following year, and short-listed candidates are interviewed in February. Those elected will be expected to contribute £50 to £200 depending on the dollar-pound rate on the 4-week scholarship (where the grant would be about £500). Hospitality in the USA is provided by the US branch of the ESU.

Post-to-post exchanges

These are organised by the **Central Bureau for Educational Visits and Exchanges,** a UK governmental agency responsible to the various British departments of education. Their aim is to develop contacts, cooperation and exchanges between British teachers and teachers overseas.

The scheme is open to all qualified British teachers from nursery schools through to universities with five or more years' experience, of which the final two years must have been with the same school or college. Posts can be exchanged for a full year, or for a term. Applications for a year's exchange have to be completed by early December, or by the end of June for spring term visits.

Exchanges are organised centrally. If a high school geography teacher from North Dakota applies to the US organisers just as another such geography teacher from Inverness applies the Central Bureau would try to arrange for them to swap jobs, perhaps even accommodation, subject to both teachers being accepted as suitable. As this might be a very hit and miss way of getting an exchange it has been suggested informally that teachers *already* in contact (say after a holiday trip or via friends and relatives) might like to submit a statement to both sets of organisers saying a link has already been established. This is the way university teachers usually swap jobs on this or on other such schemes.

Teachers return to their post upon returning home. They are seconded on full salary with all rights safeguarded. The visit counts as service for all purposes, including incremental credit. Grants from central government also cover return travel and any necessary extra cost of living allowance (a British salary will not go very far in the USA, especially not if the exchange is for central New York City!).

In addition the US authorities give each teacher a free insurance policy for sickness and accident during the period of the exchange (as the US visiting teacher in Britain would be eligible for NHS treatment).

Applications for the US/UK Teacher Exchange Schemes can be obtained by sending 12″ by 9″ stamped addressed envelope along with your name, home and institution addresses, with a note on subjects taught to:

- Teacher Exchange (USA), Central Bureau for Education Visits & Exchanges

At:
- Seymour Mews House, Seymour Mews, London W1H 9PE
- 3 Bruntsfield Crescent, Edinburgh EH10 4HD
- 16 Malone Road, Belfast BT9 5BN

School exchanges

For those teachers hardened by years of school trips, camps, outward bound and field trips the ultimate organisational experience might now be available: a UK/US school exchange. After matching, school pupils from the UK live in the homes of their US partners and attend the link school for four weeks. The US pupils return the visit either in the summer or autumn terms. It is hoped that once established links would continue between the two communities, a form of educational twinning almost.

Contact the various Central Bureau offices (see above for addresses). English and Welsh schools should contact the London office ((01) 486 5101), Scottish schools the Edinburgh office ((031) 447 8024), and Northern Irish schools the Belfast office ((0232) 664418/9)

Higher education exchanges

Full-time academics may also be eligible for Fulbright grants for head-for-head exchanges lasting a full academic year. Travel and subsistence expenses may be approved for those initiating exchanges of younger staff. Closing date is usually 1st November. Information and application forms are available from either:

- **The British Council (Higher Education Division),** 10 Spring Gardens, London SW1A 2BN ((01) 930 8466, ext. 2722), or
- **The US/UK Education Commission,** 6 Porter Street, London W1A 2LH ((01) 486 7697)

12
Staying or Returning

REMAINING IN THE USA

Most visitors to the USA, whether long or short stay, will at some point consider the possibility of staying on permanently, making the USA home, if only in the medium term. You'll need to consider:
- career implications
- family reactions
- implications for health care and retirement
- possible status − resident or citizen?

Career implications
Only *you* can judge how good an idea staying on could be for career prospects. It is possible to get locked into your US-based career structure without giving adequate consideration to moving sideways back into the UK. Who wants to get off a moving staircase if it's going steadily upwards? But remember: career implications are only one reason for staying or returning, even if they seem the most obvious.

Family reactions
These need careful consideration, both for the immediate family, presumably with you in the USA, and those back at home such as ageing parents. Whereas the side of the family back in Britain will probably be stoical (they may have assumed you'd gone for good when you set off originally) your family in the USA will react in terms of their immediate needs, fears and expectations. Most children will have settled down quite quickly and will not want to move anywhere, certainly not back to a country they hardly remember. But remember they would not want to move to the next town if they were still back in Britain, so you need to consider how much weight the grown-ups should give the views of the children. But do let them have their say, and explain why you intend to overrule them if necessary.

Perhaps more critically you'll need to ask certain questions about the family staying on:

- What are their US-based career prospects?
- Will college be an affordable option in the USA?
- Will you want them to become US citizens?
- Should you give them the option to return home at, say, 18 to make up their own minds?
- What if they return to the UK and stay on?

Health care and retirement

You'll probably just continue with your existing health plan, but what of retirement? The US social security system is getting very fragile, with no prospects of improvements as more and more people reach retirement age and the US budget deficit grows ever larger. The pensionable age is being gradually raised, but with economic restructuring pressure on people to retire earlier and earlier continues. The US military has helped promote the belief that after 20 years service, at whatever age, it's time to retire, or at least take a pension *and* start another career. Ever more people are opening an **Individual Retirement Account (IRA)**. This will allow you to supplement any government pension, but if you attempt to use the money before the agreed term you'll lose most if not all of the tax benefits. As IRAs proliferate the information about them grows. See a trusted accountant!

A word of warning: your health plan was for a limited stay (with a return to the UK always a possibility if things got dire). Is your health plan now adequate if you want to stay on a different basis? It's worth checking it out. Ask other people who've stayed on whether they changed their health care plan, or if not, do they wish they had?

Citizen status

Though the *green* card no longer exists permanent status does. If you want to change your status consult a lawyer specialising in this field, though initially you could have a look at something like Howard David Deutsch's *Getting Into America,* published by Coronet Books in 1985. It's US title suggests its wider usage: *The United States Visa and Immigration Handbook,* Random House 1984. Marrying a US citizen is the most popular reason for staying on in the USA, and it's the way that certainly makes the paperwork easiest if you arrived on a non-immigrant visa. And you won't have to return home before applying! Failing that you'll need to gain status as set out earlier in this book. Your employer will probably be the most important factor, emphasising skills needed for the US economy, and that the job won't deprive an American of a job.

Should you adopt citizenship?

For many people publicly disavowing their country of birth is one step too far. Whereas it was presumably easy for Germans fleeing the Nazis in the 1930s, for those not in exile it's probably a much more difficult decision. Fortunately taking US citizenship doesn't cancel British citizenship, except as far as the USA is concerned. British law accepts dual citizenship. US law doesn't. And if you think this a lawyer's quibble it's worth recalling that the 1812 war between Britain and the USA was over just this point (Britain press-ganged US citizens on US vessels on the high-seas saying they were still British and there was a war on against France, etc).

If you do take US citizenship and lose your British passport for an American one you could still re-enter the UK and settle down back home again. Strictly speaking you don't even need a British passport to re-enter Britain, just some means of identification (the author has used an RAC card at Heathrow before!). You'll forfeit US citizenship if you take out a British passport or run for office outside the USA (as would *any* US citizen).

There might still be a joker in the pack that you've not thought of when considering permanent residency and citizenship: **military service.** Once legally settled into the US *all* men over 18 must register (see notices on how to do this at your local US Post Office). Once the Vietnam War ended, the draft (conscription) ended. The USA now has a professional, full-time army (despite a revolutionary heritage that considered anything other than a citizens' part-time militia a start down the road to tyranny). But in times of international stress things can and do change. Even in peacetime it is an offence not to register. It is even possible that anyone liable to the draft who came back to the UK to avoid it would be liable to be handed over to the US authorities under the appropriate visiting forces act. Remember that US draft dodgers went to Canada or Sweden *not* the UK during the 1960s!

COMING BACK TO THE UK

Returning to the UK can be as great a decision as going away in the first place. For many it's even more difficult: new roots have been put down, it's always easier to stay put, and home starts to appear like the foreign country it has actually become.

What's changed?
- the government (or not as the case may be)
- the currency (coins for English £1 notes)
- TV channels (all day TV, extra channels)
- motorway network (which can be disorienting)
- the cost of everything (£1 a pint)
- very (too?) American?
- EEC integration (passport and courts)
- house prices (US urban costs in the UK southeast)

Some things haven't changed:
- the unpredictability of the weather (three good days then a thunderstorm)
- London taxis
- draught stout

And so on. These are what await someone returning after years in the USA. What will have changed if and when you get back in five or ten years?

When you are away change will continue as ever, and you'll have to meet it all at once if you return. If you'd left in 1971 and kept in touch only by telephone, Christmas cards, a quick dash back for a funeral, plus British television programmes on the PBS network, what would Britain of 1988 look like? Answer: a foreign country.

How to make contact back home
You'll need to explore as wide a variety of approaches as possible:

- Put the word out that you are interested in returning home for the right job. Let your contacts know you are thinking of moving back if the right slot opens up. Here having kept in touch will pay off. Come back to conferences (even if at your own expense) to keep a high profile, to let colleagues in your field know that you haven't fallen off the edge of the world, and perhaps as vital, to remind prospective employers you are still interested and keeping in touch.
- Read the British newspapers (as available in large universities) for any idea of what's coming vacant, who to contact (even if you are too late for particular jobs).
- Write to friends and contacts to widen your circle.
- Approach UK agencies with a CV — they may be looking for someone with US experience.

US taxation
You'll need to prove to the IRS you'll be leaving with no tax debt. If you leave fully paid up you'll be due a tax refund in due course, unless you

left at the very end of the tax year. Leaving at the right time can be as advantageous to your tax situation as getting married at the right point in the tax year can be.

UK National Insurance
If you've been out for more than three years you'll need to re-establish yourself. Employers will usually do this for you.

UK Immigration
Technically returning British citizens don't need a passport to enter the UK. Crossing from the Irish Republic to Northern Ireland you may not even see border control (though you might have to negotiate an army check point). At international airports you'll get through with either a UK or US passport, though is you are obviously not returning as a tourist UK papers, such as a birth certificate, may ease your way. An American spouse with a US passport coming in with a British spouse should get the paperwork sorted out with the UK authorities in the USA, but usually it's easier for a US passport holder to enter the UK as a 6 months tourist, changing status as per the procedure outlined by the:

- **Home Office Immigration & Nationality Department,** Lunar House, Wellesley Road, Croydon CR9 2BY ((01) 686 0688, calls taken in rotation, closing at 4 pm).

UK government leaflets HC169 and HC503 explain the rules in detail. A fiancé(e) can enter this way, but if you apply for fiancé(e) (rather than tourist) entrance you'll need to provide written proof of a planned wedding within *three* months, and the visa will be for a maximum of three months.

UK Customs and Excise
There's no need to provide the detailed listing necessary on entering the USA, but be honest and don't try to bring in restricted items (especially pets). Personal effects over 6 months old will come in duty free.

Pets
If you need to ask how much it costs to bring a pet over and to have it go through quarantine you can't afford it (a happy, helpful hint offered by the Embassy in Washington DC). By mid 1980s reckon on £600 for the quarantine alone, plus the cost of the flight. Quarantine is for 6 months, though visiting is permitted after the first two weeks.

RETURNING HOME

You can move home, find a large supermarket nearby, drive on the motorway into work, and hardly notice you've changed countries. But spirits will cost about twice as much as in the USA, blue jeans a lot more, and petrol even more again. You'll miss your US friends of course, but enjoy re-meeting your British ones. You'll enjoy good shoe shops, with width fittings for children, a range of beers, but the couldn't care less attitude of so many shop assistants will be a delight you'll soon realise you hadn't missed at all. Eating out will be less frequent, though you'll probably do it more than your British friends. The weather may be a bit of a surprise, especially the lack of both long standing snow or stable hot weather.

Salaries will seem very low: they are. People in the middle income bracket are less well off in the UK. Those lower or higher may well be better off. But holidays will probably be twice those you had in the USA. Being able to visit the continent will of course mean cheaper foreign holidays – but EEC regulations have still not reduced air fares to levels comparable to those within the USA.

Families that hated going to the USA may well hate returning. US sport, fast food, late night shopping and the swimming pool in the sunshine may all seem like paradise lost, especially for teenage children or a spouse whose career progress has been broken yet again. Fortunately pre-teen children adjust well given love, attention and food. Teenagers are something else. Moving away from friends, perhaps even a first love, can be traumatic, especially if tackled heavy handedly.

Children will have to change schools so it will help to move in sync with the natural breaks in the school year, preferably between years, ideally when a change of school would be involved anyway. If your child started school in the USA they'll be behind comparable British children, if only for having started later.

Coming back to go to university might not be a good idea without considerable organisation. Scottish students starting at English or Welsh universities with a school education one year shorter can have major difficulties, especially in technical subjects. How much less prepared will students from the USA be! Better try for British 'A' levels via a college of further education before applying for university or polytechnic. Arriving at university after such a bridge can be very profitable. And older students generally get better degrees.

If you have been on a mutual academic or teachers' exchange slotting back in again may take no time at all: children return to their old friends and a new teacher, your own car may seem much smaller than you remember (and perhaps more worse for wear) and various changes in the house, garden and neighbourhood will gradually make themselves known. But if you have been away for several years on contract or secondment you need to consider:

- US and UK tax consequences – in the year of return you may actually be eligible for tax rebates!
- UK capital gains liabilities on US investments sold off on returning home
- renewed National Insurance liability (including the implications of having missed paying in for several years)
- regaining any tax advantages on any long-held life assurance policies.

For an excellent summary of the financial implications of your eventual return to the UK see Harry Brown's *Working Abroad: The Guide to Fiscal Do's and Don'ts,* Northcote House, Plymouth, 5th edition 1986 (£6.95).

US English

The official language of the State of Illinois shall be known hereafter as the 'American' language and not as the 'English' language.

Act of Illinois Legislature 1923.

American English sprang originally from British English, and in certain ways and in certain areas retains its heritage in a form far more traditional than generally found in Britain. The speech of Appalachia can be traced back to the hills of Ulster, the Scottish borders, and the West Country. And a US performance of Shakespeare's plays is likely to involve pronunciation and intonation far more familiar to the Bard himself than anything he'd hear in Stratford today. British English has moved on from its Elizabethan stage. Only in the peripheral areas of the English-speaking world can the older, most truly Anglo-Saxon forms be found.

But US English moves on too. The simplicity of Anglo-Saxon usage has been its downfall. It simply doesn't sound sophisticated enough in an increasingly cosmopolitan age. There isn't, after all, a truly Anglo-Saxon word for 'sophisticated'! So Americans have sought to improve their standing by 'improving' their English, by which they mean using long words in ever more complex patterns. It has something to do with the rise of meritocracy, the professionalism of so much of American life, but mostly the need to sound as if you are at the cutting edge of science and progress. If regional accents in the USA carry no indication of social standing then vocabulary and syntax will have to do so instead.

A little simultaneous translation from Shakespeare may show what's involved:

Original:	*Modern USA:*
It is a tale	It is in narrative form
told by	vocalised by
an idiot,	an individual of arrested mental development
full of	emphasising the
sound and	audio and
fury,	hyperindignant components,
signifying	possessing
nothing	no meaningful insight

The impact of Latin-based words and Germanic-sounding sentences has been enormous. Today there's also computer terminology. Memories *download,* people *interface,* surely classic cases of GIGO (Garbage In, Garbage Out). 'O' level Latin will finally be of some use to help get to grips with all the prefixes: *counterurbanization, exurban,* and don't forget *post-industrial.*

The American language is indeed flexible and dynamic. You can even make things seem better by your choice of terms. Don't have a family row: enjoy an aggressive interpersonal interaction. You don't like the idea of hiring a cleaner? Then hire a domestic hygiene specialist. And that wasn't a pay-cut. That was a downward income adjustment. Video clips on MTV (the video channel) are not repeated regularly, rather they are made to withstand 'heavy rotation'! And remember: when house hunting you should be wary of living downwind of the effluent treatment plant.

Glossary

> The first Americans had ...to invent Americanisms, if only to describe the unfamiliar landscape, weather, flora, and fauna confronting them.
>
> M.L. Mencken, *The American Landscape*, 1919

AAA. American Automobile Association.

apartment. Flat.

area code. Dialling (STD) code.

baggage. Luggage.

bathroom. Toilet (WC) but also known as 'the john' (from seventeenth-century English); 'the head' (naval bulkhead); 'washroom'; 'comfort station'; or 'restroom'.

billion. Thousand million.

biscuit. Scone-like roll.

broiled. Grilled.

brownbag. (as in 'we'll brownbag it'). To work through lunch with each person bringing their own packed lunch (traditionally in a brown bag).

busy signal. Engaged tone.

BYO. Bring your own (bottle).

cable. Message. Telegram (now 'telemessage' in UK).

call collect. Reverse the charges.

can. Tin (food).

Canuck. Canadian (derogatory).

chaser. Long drink (usually beer) to follow a spirit.

check. Bill (restaurant).

checkroom. Cloakroom (but *not* a WC).

closet. Cupboard (usually built in).

coach class. 2nd or tourist class.

comfort station. Roadside toilets.

community chest. A local fund for neighbourhood charities.

community college. Publicly funded college for local people offering vocational or pre-university courses, similar to further education colleges in Britain.

condominium ('condo'). Flats sold to sitting tenants, or purpose built with housing association-like tenancy but commercially run.

cookie. Biscuit.

corn. Maize.

Daylight Saving Time. Summer time.

detour (on sign). Diversion.

diaper. Nappy.

divided highway. Dual carriageway.

Dixie. The South (south of Mason-*Dixon* line).

draft, the. Conscription.

dual citizenship. Having citizenship of two countries at once (illegal for US citizens).

duplex. A two-floored apartment.

easy over. Eggs fried both sides.

El. The elevated railway (in Chicago).

elevator. Lift.

expressway. Motorway.

fall. Autumn.

FDIC. Federal Deposit Insurance Corporation (government agency insuring bank deposits).

FHA. Federal Housing Administration (agency that insures new construction mortgages).

fifth. Bottle of spirits (⅕ US gallon).

first name. Christian name.

food stamps. Coupons bought by poor people at below face value for use in food shops at face value.

garage sale. A car boot sale in one's own driveway.

garbage can. Dustbin.

gas. Petrol.

gearshift. Manual transmission.

general delivery. Poste restante.

GI Bill. Popular name for Serviceman's Readjustment Act (1944) entitling veterans to post discharge benefits, especially payment of college fees.

go, to. Take away, carry out.

GOP. Republican Party ('Grand Old Party').

green card. Permit to live in USA (no longer green).

happy hour. Half-price drinks in late afternoon.

help. Servants (particularly a southern euphemism for black servants).

hockey. Ice hockey (not field hockey).

hood. Bonnet of car.

hose. Tights.

icebox. Refrigerator.

IRS. Internal Revenue Service.

INS. Immigration & Naturalization Service.

JAP. 'Jewish-American-Princess' (or any spoilt rich girl).

jay walking. Illegal crossing of street.

jello. Jelly.

jelly. Jam.

klutz. Socially inept person.

limey. A Brit.

loaded. Drunk.

long distance call. Trunk call.

mailgram. Telemessage.

Martini. 3 parts vermouth, 1 part gin +olive.

men working. Road works.

mezzanine. Floor between main floors.

night letter. Overnight telegram (now 'telemessage' in UK).

no passing. No overtaking.

NORAID. Northern Irish Aid (IRA fundraiser).

NRA. National Rifle Association (major gun lobby).

observatory. Viewing platform.

Okie. Farmers from Oklahoma (who fled to California in the 1930s).

one way (ticket). Single ticket.

overpass. Flyover.

pants. Trousers.

pavement. Road surface (tarmac).

penny sale. Special offer where

second item costs only lc (essentially two for cost of one).

person to person. Personal call.

phone booth. Call box.

plaza. Open square.

poison ivy. Similar to Virginia creeper (but poisonous).

preppy. Lifestyle associated with young people of social elite.

railroad crossing. Level crossing.

rain check. A promise to take up an invitation at a later date.

ramp. Motorway sliproad.

realtor. Estate agent.

redcap. Porter (airport or railway station).

redneck. Right-wing blue-collar worker.

roadway. Carriageway.

roundtrip (ticket). Return.

rotary. Roundabout.

school. Any institute of education (especially university).

SEC. Securities and Exchange Commission (stock exchange watchdog).

sidewalk. Pavement.

soccer. Football.

special delivery. Express post.

stand in line. Queue.

store. Shop.

straight. Neat (liquor).

streetcar. Tram.

subway. Underground railway-/tube.

sunny side up. Eggs fried without being turned over.

3.2 beer. A fairly weak beer with 3.2% alcohol (legalised from the 7th April 1933, the end of Prohibition), still often the only beer legally available in certain States.

toll-free number. Free call (1-800 prefix).

traffic circle. Roundabout.

trailer. Caravan.

tramway. Cable car.

treaty investor. A substantial investor seeking residence on a non-immigrant basis, and coming from a country with a reciprocal treaty.

trunk. Boot of car.

TVA. Tennessee Valley Authority (regional development agency and power company in southern Appalachians).

two weeks. Fortnight.

twofers. Two for price of one.

underpass. Subway (pedestrian only).

unlisted number. Ex-directory.

VA. Veterans' Administration.

veteran. Anyone honourably discharged from the US forces (including coastguard).

VCR. Video (cassette recorder).

WASP. White Anglo-Saxon Protestant.

windshield. windscreen.

wire. Telegram (now 'telemessage' in UK).

WPA. Work Projects Administration (a make-work agency 1939- 43).

yield (on sign)Give way.

yuppy. 'Young upwardly mobile professional'.

zip code. 5 digit post code.

Statutory Public Holidays

New Year	1st January
Martin Luther King's Birthday	16th January (most States)
Washington's Birthday	22nd February
Memorial Day	Last Monday in May (46 States)
Independence Day	4th July
Labor Day	First Monday in September
Columbus Day	Second Monday of October (32 States)
Veteran's Day	11th November ('Armistice Day')
Thanksgiving	Fourth Thursday in November
Christmas Day	25th December.

Beware Public holidays are State *not* federally authorised. Most States give all the above holidays, which are also enjoyed by federal employees throughout the USA. Lincoln's Birthday is observed in northern but not southern States.

Weights and Measures

US imperial measures of length are the same as in the UK *but* measures of capacity are somewhat different: the US gallon is *smaller* than the British equivalent (1 US gallon = 0.83 UK gallon); the US hundredwieght (cwt) is smaller than the British (being 100 lb rather than 112 lb); a US ton is short (2,000 lb rather than 2,240 lb, whereas a metric tonne is 2,204 lb).

All imperial and US measures are gradually being replaced by metric (SI) measures, in theory if not in people's minds. As in the UK the change-over is long and drawn out, in comparison to Canada where it was short and sweet.

British visitors who think of themselves as firmly non-metric may find to their surprise that they are more metric than they thought when confronted with US measures. The author once mistook a 12 degrees weather report for 12 degrees Celsius rather than 12 degrees Fahrenheit and almost froze.

Consulates in the USA

Australia
- 635 5th Ave, New York, NY ((212) 245 4000)
- 1601 Massachusetts Ave NW, Washington DC ((202) 797 3159)

Canada
- 1251 Ave of the Americas, New York, NY ((212) 586 2400)
- 1746 Massachusetts Ave NW, Washington DC ((202) 785 1400)

Ireland
- 580 5th Ave, New York, NY ((212) 382 2525)
- 2234 Massachusetts Ave NW, Washington DC ((202) 483 7639)

New Zealand
- Suite 530, 5th Ave, New York, NY ((212) 586 6060)
- 19 Observatory Circle NW, Washington DC ((202) 265 1721)

South Africa
- 425 Park Ave, New York, NY ((212) 838 1700)
- 3051 Massachusetts Ave NW, Washington DC ((202) 232 4400)

UK
- 225 Peachtree St NE, Atlanta, GA ((404) 524 5856)
- 120 Montgomery St, San Francisco, CA ((415) 981 3030)
- 845 3rd Ave, New York, NY ((212) 752 8400)
- 3100 Massachusetts Ave NW, Washington DC ((202) 462 1340)

State Tourist Offices

Most State tourist offices listed below are in the State capital (for instance, Albany for New York, Annapolis for Maryland), but local offices may be found, especially at drive-in rest areas on entering a State by freeway. The State road maps alone are worth an enquiry.

	Numbers	Toll-free numbers
Alabama		1-800-252 2262
Alaska	(907) 465 2010	
Arizona	(602) 255 3618	
Arkansas		1-800-643 8383
California	(916) 322 1396	
Colorado	(303) 892 1112	
Connecticut	(203) 566 3977	(or in north east 1-800-842 7492)
Delaware	(302) 736 4271	1-800-441 8846
District of Columbia	(202) 789 7000	
Florida	(904) 487 1462	
Georgia	(404) 656 3590	
Hawaii	(808) 923 1811	
Idaho	(208) 334 2470	1-800-635 7820
Illinois	(312) 793 2094	
Indiana	(307) 232 8860	
Iowa	(515) 281 3100	
Kansas	(913) 296 2009	
Kentucky	(502) 564 4930	
Louisiana	(504) 925 3860	
Maine	(207) 289 2423	
Maryland	(301) 269 3517	
Massachusetts	(617) 727 3201	
Michigan	(517) 373 0670	1-800-248 5700

Minnesota	(612) 296 5029	1-800-328 1461
Mississippi		1-800-647 2290
Missouri	(314) 751 4133	
Montana	(406) 449 2654	1-800-548 3390
Nebraska	(402) 471 3796	
Nevada	(702) 885 4322	
New Hampshire	(603) 271 2343	
New Jersey	(609) 827 6230	1-800-545 2040
New York	(518) 474 4116	(in northeast 1-800-225 5697)
North Carolina	(919) 733 4171	
North Dakota	(701) 224 2525	1-800-441 8846
Ohio	(614) 466 8844	1-800-282 5393
Oklahoma	(405) 521 2406	(locally 1-800-652 6552)
Oregon	(503) 373 1200	1-800-547 7842
Pennsylvania	(717) 787 5453	1-800-237-4363
Rhode Island	(401) 277 2601	(northeast states only 1-800-556 2484)
South Carolina	(605) 773 3301	1-800-843 1930
Tennessee	(615) 741 2158	
Texas	(512) 475 5956	
Utah	(801) 533 5681	
Vermont	(802) 828 3236	
Virginia	(804) 786 2051	
Washington	(206) 753 5600	
West Virginia	(304) 348 2286	
Wisconsin	(608) 266 2161	
Wyoming	(307) 777 7777	

The **United States Travel and Tourism Administration** can be contacted on a toll-free hotline within the USA on 1-800-255 3050. In the UK their office is 22 Sackville Street, LONDON W1X 2EA ((01) 439 7433). Some States are represented in the UK, though they usually deal only with the travel trade:

- **Hawaii:** Marble Arch House, Seymour St, LONDON W1 ((01) 402 2371)
- **New York State:** 25 Bedford Square, LONDON, WC1B 2HG ((01) 323 0648)
- **Oklahoma:** PO Box 126, HEMEL HEMPSTEAD, Herts HP3 OAZ ((0442) 214621)

More Useful Addresses

Counselling: foreign employment
- Personnel International Ltd,
  PO Box 240
  ST PETER PORT
  Guernsey
  Channel Islands

- Professional & Executive Recruitment Overseas
  4-5 Grosvenor Place,
  LONDON SWIX 7SB

Visas and permits
- Blair Consular Service Ltd,
  10 Fairfax Avenue,
  STAINES,
  Middlesex

Packing and Overseas Removals
- British Association of Removers,
  279 Gray's Inn Road,
  LONDON WC1

- Graham Masters and Co. Ltd,
  Staplehurst Road,
  SITTINGBOURNE,
  Kent

- Neale Wilkinson Ltd,
  78 Stratford Broadway
  LONDON E15

Contributions from those overseas

- **DHSS** (Overseas Branch),
  Benton Park Road,
  NEWCASTLE-UPON-TYNE NE98 1YX

Further Reading

Bloom, A, *The Closing of the American Mind,* Simon & Schuster, New York 1987

Bradbury, M, *Stepping Westward,* Arena, London 1984

Brogan, H, *The Pelican History of the United States of America,* Penguin, Harmondsworth 1986

Brookeman, C, *American Culture and Society since the 1930s,* Macmillan, Basingstoke 1985

Brown, H, *Working Abroad,* Northcote House, Plymouth 1986

Burgess, A, *The Expatriate's Guide,* Neville Russell, London 1986

Cranfield, I, *The Traveller's Handbook,* Heinemann, London 1980

Davies, R A, *A Layman's Guide to Profitable Letting,* Jofleur, Watlington 1986

Deutsch, H D, *Getting into America,* Hodder & Stoughton, Sevenoaks 1985

Eastway, N A and Young, D. *Expatriate Tax and Investment Guide,* Longman, London 1986

Farrell P, *How to Buy a Business,* Kogan Page, London 1983

Fodor's America 1987, Hodder & Stoughton, London 1986

Fox, K, *Metropolitan America: Urban Life in the US 1945-1980,* Macmillan, Basingstoke, 1985.

Griffin, S and Calder S, *Traveller's Survival Kit — USA and Canada,* Vacation Work, Oxford 1985

Golzen, G, *Working Abroad,* Kogan Page, London 1987

Grossman, S, *Have Kids Will Travel,* Christopher Helm, London 1987

Haslam, D, *Travelling with Kids,* Macdonald, London 1987

Leppard, D, *The Directory of Jobs and Careers Abroad,* Vacation Work, Oxford 1987

Lodge, D, *Changing Places,* Penguin, Harmondsworth 1975

Moss, M and G, *Handbook for Women Travellers,* Piatkus, London 1987

Owen, D, *High School,* Viking, New York 1981

Reich, R B, *The Next American Frontier,* Penguin, Harmondsworth 1984

Rosenberg, S, *American Economic Development Since 1945,* Macmillan, Basingstoke 1985

Ryan, D S, *America: A Guide to the Experience,* Kozmik, London 1986

Wicks, R and Schultz, F, *Long Stays in America,* David & Charles, Newton Abbot 1986

Index

Also available from Northcote House:

New

How to Live & Work in Australia
Laura Veltman

The Australian High Commission recently reported further rises in the number of people applying to visit Australia — both as tourists, and as immigrants. This new How To... title is the only title available which explains how to become a temporary or permanent Australian resident, how to beat the red tape, and how to qualify under the crucial 'points' system. Australia, like most countries today, has tough screening processes; the would-be emigrant will really need the jaunty but expert advice uniquely available in this new book.

Contents First the good news, great expectations, Australia — the making of a nation, attitudes Down Under, going to Australia: how will you get in?, foreign qualifications and studying in Australia, business migration — locations and incentives, money and making it, Australian taxation and company law, housing and property, driving in Australia, playing Down Under, Australian health and welfare, Australian education, taking it all with you, Oz-Speak: An introduction to Australian Slang, further reading, useful addresses and contacts, index.

Readership/markets All would-be emigrants to Australia, short-stay and long-stay visitors, Public, business and institutional libraries, personnel departments and careers offices, recruitment consultants, government, consular and other official offices.

Laura Veltman is a journalist specialising in Australian migrant affairs. She has contributed to *The Australian, The Sunday Times, The Observer* and other leading periodicals on Australian matters.

£5.95 pb. 215 x 135mm. 160pp Illustrated
0 7463 0331 9 Northcote House

Complete Guide to American Bed and Breakfast
Rik and Nancy Barnes

Discover the *personal* way to see America. This revised and expanded second edition invites you to explore more than 1600 inns across the country. From converted old mansions in New England to rustic hunting lodges out West, inns reflect the flavour of their region. Divided into sections alphabetically by state and city, listings include addresses, phone numbers, and innkeepers' names, current rates, restrictions (such as no smoking), and special features. Maps of each state pinpoint the locations of each inn. An appendix provides a complete listing of American B & B associations and reservation agencies.

£11.95 pb. 230 x 145mm. 650pp. Illustrated
0 88289 649 0 Pelican Publishing Co.

Working Abroad?
The Guide to Fiscal and Financial Do's and Don'ts
Harry Brown

As many as 2 million British citizens are now believed to be working expatriates. About one in ten return to the UK each year, and as many again depart abroad. Completely revised and updated, this new edition of the best-seller **Working Abroad?** meets a real need for information and advice crucial to every expatriate — and which is otherwise difficult or expensive to get. First published by the *Financial Times* in 1977, **Working Abroad?** has established itself as the authentic handbook of expatriates.

'This is worth reading before you go, while you're there, and when you come back' *British Business*
'New edition of the now classic **Working Abroad**?' *Arab Times*
'This book is a mine of information and is a MUST for anyone to read before they make costly mistakes.' *Homes and Travel Abroad*
● Fully revised new edition
● 200,000 copies already sold
● Every expatriate's 'bible'

Contents UK taxation and what it means for expatriates; banking for expatriates; children's education; expatriate investment; leasing your home in the UK; life assurance for expatriates and their families; pension planning; preparing to return home; UK social security and national insurance; index.

Harry Brown, described by *The Times* as inimitable, is generally regarded as Britain's pre-eminent specialist on expatriate matters. He speaks with enormous professional authority, and enjoys a huge personal following among the expatriate community worldwide. He is also author of the best-selling **Retiring Abroad?**

£6.95 pb. 210 x 149mm. 160pp. Illustrated
0 7463 0383 1 Northcote House

New Edition

The Complete Guide to Bed & Breakfasts, Inns & Guesthouses in the United States and Canada
Pamela Lanier

As the bed-and-breakfast movement continues to grow, so does Pamela Lanier's essential handbook. This new edition includes over 3000 individual annotated listings. In addition to being the most complete and up-to-date B & B book on the market, **The Complete Guide** maintains its reputation as the most unique guide by adding even more lists of inns by speciality-gourmet food, historic setting, family fun, skiing, or rooms for under $30 a night.

£12.95 pb. 220 x 140mm. 640pp.
0 912528 61 3 John Muir Publications

The Marmac Guides to American Cities

The **Marmac Guides** are designed for the traveller who wants comprehensive information in an easy-to-use, clear, bold format. Each guide highlights the essentials of the community and items of special note to tourists, including transportation, lodging, restaurants, nightlife, sightseeing, museums, galleries, shopping, sports and excursions. They are especially useful to business travellers. Key area maps are placed at the beginning of each book for reference. Other maps plot down-town streets, in-town and out-of-town tours, and special interest areas. In addition, special sections are included on self guided tours, one-day excursions, and information for new residents. Choose a **Marmac Guide** and you'll get to the heart of America.

Each 207 × 134mm. All priced £7.95, paperback
Titles in the series are as follows:
A Marmac Guide to Atlanta, *Schemmel & McDonald*
0 939944 27 8
A Marmac Guide to Houston and Galveston, *Young*
0 939944 03 0
A Marmac Guide to Los Angeles, *Chapman* 0 939944 14 6
A Marmac Guide to New Orleans, *Cary and McCarthy*
0 939944 28 6
A Marmac Guide to Philadelphia, *Ronberg* 0 939944 29 4
Pelican Publishing Co.

Pelican Guide to Historic Homes and Sites of Revolutionary America
Volume 1: New England
Adelaide Hechtlinger

'This guide covers Maine, Vermont, New Hampshire, Rhode Island, Massachusetts and Connecticut... very useful for the tourist who wishes to plan an itinerary to visit these states' landmarks dating from the Revolutionary epoch.' *American Reference Books Annual.*

£4.95 pb. 128pp. Illustrated
0 88289 090 5 Pelican Publishing Co

Pelican Guide to New Orleans
Tommy Griffin

'The book is written in a chatty and entertaining manner by a man who is a native of New Orleans and knows the city well... Because it provides an excellent overview, this book should be read from cover to cover by anyone planning to visit the Crescent City for the first time. Because it includes recent information, it is a must for the frequent visitor as well.' *American Reference Books Annual*

£5.95 pb. 160pp. Illustrated
0 88289 010 7 Pelican Publishing Co.

New

Pelican Guide to the Shenandoah
Regina Pierce and Sharon Yackso

Pelican Guide to the Shenandoah takes the visitor on a tour 'up the valley', including stops at Winchester, Front Royal, Luray, Staunton and Charlottesville. Arranged geographically by community, each chapter highlights the history of the area. Accurate information on points of interest, recreational activities, shopping, dining, lodging, and seasonal events, plus phone numbers and addresses for each area are also included.

£7.95 pb. 210 x 140mm. 128pp. Illustrated, photographs, maps
0 88289 652 0 Pelican Publishing Co.

New

American Southwest in Your Pocket
Richard Harris

Venture beyond the reach of interstate highways, where traditional Native American, Spanish colonial and pioneer communities still endure alongside futuristic space research sites. In between Santa Fe style and Las Vegas glitz, discover ancient ruins, frontier ghost towns, volcanos and giant sand dunes, cool mountains, vast deserts and canyonlands that surpass imagination. This trip, designed for motorists with supplemental information for non-campers, covers areas of New Mexico, Colorado, Utah, Nevada and Arizona, as well as the lands of the Navajo, Pueblo, Zuni, Hopi, Paiute and Apache people. Side trips by horse, boat, raft, jeep, bicycle and narrow-gauge train are suggested. A special section for winter travellers discusses the Sonora Desert, Mexican border areas and skiing in the southwest.

£4.95 pb. 205 x 115mm. 136pp. Illustrated
1 85373 046 7 Northcote House

New

Alaska in Your Pocket
Pamela Lanier

America's last frontier. Alaska is the ultimate vacation destination for growing numbers of adventurous motorists. This tour takes you north from the US border along the scenic AlCan Highway through the Canadian Yukon to Anchorage, Alaska's largest city. Explore the beaches, historic towns and wildlife areas of Alaska's southern coastline on foot, on horseback or by boat. Visit the Fairbanks gold rush country and the vast wilderness of Denali National Park, the premier wildlife viewing preserve in North America. Return by ferry down the Inside Passage for a three-day cruise along the continent's beautiful northwest coast. This itinerary is designed for RV enthusiasts and automobile travellers, including non-campers. A special section tells how to see Alaska by public transportation.

£4.95 pb. 205 x 115mm. 136pp. Illustrated
1 85373 041 6 Northcote House

Also available from Northcote House:

New

All-Suite Hotels
Pamela Lanier

This unique guide selects hotels in the USA that won't rent you *just* a room. The 600 all-suite hotels described offer homeliness, comfort and plenty of space — all for the same price as a conventional hotel room. Separate living areas and bedrooms, kitchen facilities, complimentary breakfasts and cocktail hours, and many more conveniences make the 'suite alternative' perfect for families, business people and anyone planning an extended stay.

Pamela Lanier's descriptions include detailed directions to each hotel, as well as complete information on special features and amenities.

£11.95 pb. 220 x 140mm. Illustrated
0 912528 70 2 John Muir Publications

New Edition

Elegant Small Hotels
Pamela Lanier

A new style of elegant small hotels is emerging in the USA — hotels characterising the grace and charm of yesteryear's European tradition while providing sophisticated accommodations for today's demanding traveller. Pamela Lanier provides business travellers as well as leisure guests with detailed information and photographs of 120 outstanding hotels. Particular emphasis is given to hotels with business service centres on the property, an elegant ambience, valet service, exotic decors, spa and sport facilities, quality entertainment and the distinctive touches that transform your stay into a vacation to remember. Complete with a new 8 page full-colour section.

£13.95 pb. 254 x 178mm. 150pp. Illustrated
0 912528 77 X John Muir Publications

Small Hotels of California
Bill Gleeson

Small Hotels of California is a selective guide to the best of California's most charming small hotels and wayside inns. This remarkable edition is a popular guide and ideas book for the discriminating traveller. The author has selected a total of 55 small hotels throughout California including the North Coast, the Wine Country, the Bay Area, the Delta, the Mother Lode, the Sierra, the South Coast and Southern California that will guarantee a stay to remember.

£7.95 pb. 153 x 228mm. 134pp. Illustrated
0 87701 293 8 Chronicle Books